READ, LEARN and DISCOVER

Jewish Holiday Cycle, Jewish Prayer Cycle
Torah Cycle, Jewish Life Cycle

by Sol Scharfstein
illustrated by Arthur Friedman

KTAV PUBLISHING HOUSE, INC.

copyright 1993 © KTAV Publishing House, Inc.
ISBN 978-0-88125-478-5
Printed in China

TABLE OF CONTENTS

INTRODUCTION

A cycle is a series of events, holidays, or celebrations that are repeated in a regular order or sequence. The planets in our solar system circle through space in a cycle. Plants and flowers grow and die in a regular cycle. Going to school and sports programs also follow a special cycle.

Many things that shape our every day lives follow a repeated order - a cycle. The Jewish religion has many celebrations and religious practices that follow a cycle.

"Read, Learn and Discover" will teach you about four different cycles in Judaism: Holiday Cycle, Torah Cycle, Prayer Cycle and Life Cycle.

In this book you will learn many important facts about your religion and its celebrations. Most of these have been observed for thousands of years. This is the chain of Jewish tradition that ties us to past generations. These celebrations will bring you closer to God and enrich your homes and your lives with their message.

In the Jewish Holiday Cycle section you will become familiar with the Jewish holidays, their history and how to celebrate them in your synagogue and in your home.

The Torah contains the beginning history of Jewish people and some of its early laws. Each year we read the Torah from beginning to end. The Torah Cycle section will teach you about the Torah and ceremonies that surround and honor it. In addition, you will learn how to participate and become a part of a Torah ceremony.

The Prayer Cycle section will help you to understand some of the rituals that take place in the synagogue and in your home. Prayer has the power to make you a better and more caring person. As you learn more about Jewish prayer you will find it easier to understand and take part in prayer ceremonies.

At certain points in your life, from the time you are born, you will celebrate "personal" events. Most of these occasions will be happy ones. In the Life Cycle section you will learn about some of these observances and how to take part in the ceremonies.

Many of these "personal" events are thousands of years old and were celebrated by your ancestors wherever they lived. When you observe these "personal" events you become part of the historical chain that stretches from Mt. Sinai to you.

Now it is your turn to "Read, Learn and Discover" your Jewish heritage so that you can become an educated link in the chain of Jewish tradition.

Sol Scharfstein

THE HEBREW CALENDAR הַלּוּחַ הָעִבְרִי

Our earth is part of the solar system. Just like the other planets we twirl around space as we circle the sun.

The calendar we use in our daily life is based upon the revolution of our planet around the sun. The Jewish calendar is a lunar, or moon, calendar. The Jewish calendar is called a Luach in Hebrew. It divides the time according to the cycles of the moon.

Our ancient rabbis measured time by using the moon's journey around the earth as a basic calendar unit.

They called 29–30 days, from full moon to full moon, a month. The Hebrew word for "month" is Chodesh. Twelve full moons, or months, are called a Shanah (year).

But nature is not always perfectly mathematical. The ancients found out that the moon year was not in sync with the sun year. The moon months could not keep up with the seasons. After a while Rosh Hashanah would be in the spring instead of the autumn. Passover could end up in the winter instead of spring. It could become very confusing.

After much thought, the Jewish mathematicians found an answer. They added an extra month to certain years so that the moon and the sun year were on the same track.

These special years are called leap years. This adjustment made the months of the Jewish calendar moon months, and the year became solar, or sun, year.

When there is a leap year, the extra month is added after Adar. The extra month is called Adar Sheni, or Adar the Second.

The Luach, just like the English calendar, has twelve months. The Hebrew names of the months come from the Babylonian calendar. Here are the Hebrew names for each of the months; with each Chodesh you will find the Jewish holiday that is celebrated in that month.

תִּשְׁרֵי	Tishri—Rosh Hashanah, Yom Kippur, Sukkot, Simchat Torah	נִיסָן	Nisan—Passover, Yom HaShoah
חֶשְׁוָן	Cheshvan	אִיָּר	Iyar—Yom HaZakron, Yom Ha'Atzmaut, Lag B'Omer
כִּסְלֵו	Kislev—Chanukah	סִיוָן	Sivan—Shavuot
טֵבֵת	Tevet	תַּמּוּז	Tammuz
שְׁבָט	Shevat—Tu Bishvat	אָב	Av—Tisha B'Av
אֲדָר	Adar—Purim	אֱלוּל	Elul

YOUR HEBREW WORD LIST

לוּחַ	Luach	Calendar
חֹדֶשׁ	Chodesh	New (moon), a month
שָׁנָה	Shanah	Year
אֲדָר שֵׁנִי	Adar sheni	Adar 2
לְבָנָה	L'vah-nah	Moon

CHOOSE YOUR ANSWER FROM THE WORD LIST
Write your answer in English or in Hebrew.

1. The time from full moon to full moon is called a _____.

2. Twelve Chadashim equals one _____.

3. The _____ is a guide to the Jewish holidays and the Torah readings during the year.

4. The extra month in a leap year is called _____.

5. On some nights the _____ is full and round, and on some nights it is just a tiny slice.

רֹאשׁ חֹדֶשׁ

WHY did our ancestors place observers on the mountaintops around Jerusalem?

BECAUSE our ancestors needed to keep track of the moon.

Sharp-eyed observers were placed on mountaintops to await the appearance of the new moon. As soon as it appeared they rushed to the Sanhedrin in Jerusalem. "We testify that we have seen the new moon," they swore. Then the Sanhedrin officially proclaimed a new moon and runners were sent to light fires on the mountaintops surrounding Jerusalem.

As soon a the signals were seen, the inhabitants of other towns lighted their fires. In a short time the signals reached all the towns in Israel. Thus, the new moon, Rosh Chodesh, was officially begun.

HOW can you figure out the number of the Hebrew year?

THERE is an easy formula.
   If you wish to figure out the number of the Hebrew year, subtract 1240 from the civil year. Then add 5000. The Hebrew year for 1993 would be:

$$
\begin{array}{r}
1993 \\
-1240 \\
\hline
753 \\
+5000 \\
\hline
5753
\end{array}
$$

That is the year if you are figuring it between January 1 and Rosh Hashanah. If you are figuring it between Rosh Hashanah and December 31, add one more year.

THE SHABBAT שַׁבָּת

The Torah tells us that God created the world in six days. On the seventh day God rested. These seven days were the very first week in all of history.

God blessed the seventh day and made it special because it was the day of resting from the work of creation. God called the seventh day Shabbat.

The Torah tells us how to make the Shabbat special. On Shabbat we remember that God created the world and rested on the seventh day. We, too, rest on Shabbat. For us it is a day of prayer and gladness. On Shabbat we go to synagogue, visit friends, read, and have family fun.

Shabbat starts on Friday evening with the lighting of the candles and the reciting of the Kiddush. You recite the Kiddush over challah and wine.

Shabbat morning everybody goes to synagogue. You meet your friends and neighbors. You wish them "Shabbat Shalom".

In the synagogue you read prayers from the Siddur. You listen to the cantor sing.

During the service the Torah is taken from the Aron Kodesh. Someone reads from the Torah.

Shabbat ends with the Havdalah ceremony. You recite blessings over a Havdalah candle, a cup of wine, and spices.

Shabbat is over for another week. You are rested and happy. Now you are ready for another six days of fun, study, and work.

YOUR HEBREW WORD LIST

הַבְדָּלָה	Havdalah	"Separation" (prayer at end of Shabbat)
סִדּוּר	Siddur	Prayerbook
חַלָּה	Challah	Sabbath and holiday bread
חַזָּן	Chazzan	Cantor
שַׁבָּת	Shabbat	The seventh day of the week, a day of rest

CHOOSE YOUR ANSWER FROM THE WORD LIST
Write your answer in English or in Hebrew.

1. God called the seventh day _____.

2. You recite the Kiddush over _____ and wine.

3. In the synagogue the _____ sings the prayers.

4. Shabbat prayers are found in the _____.

5. The _____ ceremony signals the end of the Shabbat.

START

MYSTERY MESSAGE
Use the code and find the message.

S	V	A
E	H	D
T	N	O

L	B	I
C	R	M
W	E	Y

שַׁבָּת שָׁלוֹם!

HOW do you greet people on Shabbat?

WHEN you meet a Jewish acquaintance, whether at the synagogue or outside you greet them by saying, "Shabbat Shalom," (Have a good Sabbath). You can also use the Yiddish greeting, "Gooten Shabbas."

9

ASERET Y'MAY T'SHUVAH עֲשֶׂרֶת יְמֵי תְּשׁוּבָה

The Aseret Y'may T'shuvah, the Ten Days of Repentance, celebrate the beginning of the Jewish New Year. The Aseret Y'may T'shuvah begin with the holiday of Rosh Hashanah and end ten days later with Yom Kippur.

Rosh means "new" and Shanah means "year." Together the two Hebrew words mean New Year.

Rosh Hashanah is a serious holiday. You go to the synagogue and pray for a year of good health and peace. On Rosh Hashanah you think about the good things you did in the past year. You also promise yourself that in the year to come you will try to become a better person.

On Rosh Hashanah we do T'shuvah, repentance. We ask God to forgive us for any wrongs we have done to other people and to ourselves. The Hebrew word for "repentance" is T'shuvah.

Rosh Hashanah starts on the first day of the month of Tishri.

In the synagogue we use a special prayerbook called a Machzor. The word Machzor comes from the Hebrew word *chazor*, which means "to repeat."

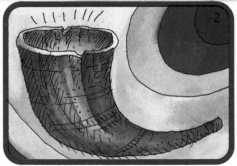

Another name for Rosh Hashanah is Yom T'ruah, "the day of the blowing of the shofar." The shofar is a ram's horn, and the sound reminds all Jews to return to Torah and to good deeds.

At home we recite Kiddush over a round challah filled with sweet raisins.
We pray that our lives during the coming year will be sweet and unending just like the round challah.

At the table everyone dips some of the challah and a slice of apple into honey and recites a special blessing. We ask God to send us a Shanah Tovah, "a year of sweetness and health."

Yom Kippur is a day of fasting and prayer. The services start with the Kol Nidre prayer. In this prayer we ask God for forgiveness for all promises that we forgot to keep.

Yom Kippur ends with the Neelah service. At the end of the Neelah service the shofar is blown. The Aseret Y'may T'shuvah are over. We hope that God has listened to our prayers and will send us a year of health and peace.

10

YOUR HEBREW WORD LIST

שׁוֹפָר	Shofar	Ram's horn
רֹאשׁ הַשָּׁנָה	Rosh Hashanah	The Start of the New Year
מַחֲזוֹר	Machzor	Prayerbook used on High Holy Days
עֲשֶׂרֶת יְמֵי תְּשׁוּבָה	Aseret Y'may T'shuvah	The Ten Days of Repentance— the ten-day period from Rosh Hashanah to Yom Kippur
יוֹם כִּפּוּר	Yom Kippur	Day of Atonement

CHOOSE YOUR ANSWER FROM THE WORD LIST
Write your answer in English or in Hebrew.

1. The prayers for Rosh Hashanah and Yom Kippur are found in the _____.

2. The ten-day period between Rosh Hashanah and Yom Kippur is called _____.

3. Another name for Rosh Hashanah and Yom Kippur is Yom Truah. We call it Yom T'ruah because of the blowing of the _____.

4. The holiday of _____ is a time for fasting.

5. _____ means "head of the year."

לְשָׁנָה טוֹבָה תִּכָּתֵבוּ

HOW do you greet people on Rosh Hashanah?

DURING Rosh Hashanah it is customary for people to greet each other with a New Year wish "L'shanah Tovah Tikatevu"—"May you be written down for a happy New Year."

YOU CAN also use the phrase "Shanah Tovah Oo'metukah"—"May you have a sweet and happy New Year."

THE YIDDISH greeting is "Ah Gooten Nei Yahr," which means, "Have a good New Year."

תְּקִיעוֹת

HOW many types of shofar blasts are blown on Rosh Hashanah?

THERE are three types of shofar blasts, known as T'kee'ot, blown on Rosh Hashanah.
1. T'kiah—a straight, unbroken blast that ends sharply.
2. Shevarim—three broken sounds, like a shiver.
3. T'ruah—a group of nine short notes.

According to the rabbis, one hundred different T'kee'ot should be blown during Rosh Hashanah services.

SUKKOT סֻכּוֹת

The Hebrews wandered through the desert for forty years before they reached the Land of Israel. The wanderers had no time to build houses. They built booths that could easily be moved. These booths were called sukkot. The sukkot were covered with leaves to shade the Hebrews from the hot desert sun.

The sukkah also reminds us of the harvest season in ancient Israel. The Jewish farmers built sukkot in the fields to shade them from the hot sun.

Sukkot starts on the 15th day of Tishri.

Five days after Yom Kippur comes the holiday of Sukkot, the Feast of Booths.

A sukkah is a booth covered with a roof of leafy branches.

We decorate the inside of the sukkah with fruits, and vegetables. The growing things are a reminder of the harvest in ancient Israel.

A blessing is recited over a Lulav and Etrog. These are for the harvest in Israel.

A Lulav is a branch from a palm tree. It is tied to Aravot and Hadasim.

An Etrog looks like a lemon and comes from a citron tree. The Etrog, Lulav, Hadasim and Aravot are called the "four kinds".

After Sukkot comes the holiday of Simchat Torah.

YOUR HEBREW WORD LIST

סֻכּוֹת	**Sukkot**	**Feast of Booths**
לוּלָב	**Lulav**	**Palm leaf**
אֶתְרוֹג	**Etrog**	**Citron fruit**
סֻכָּה	**Sukkah**	**A booth made out of branches**
עֲרָבוֹת	**Aravot**	**Willow branches**
הֲדַסִּים	**Hadasim**	**Myrtle branches**

CHOOSE YOUR ANSWER FROM THE WORD LIST
Write your answer in English or in Hebrew.

1. Another name for _____ is the Feast of Booths.

2. A _____ looks like a lemon.

3. The _____ comes from a palm tree.

4. The ancient Jewish farmers built a _____ to shelter them from the sun.

5. Parts of four different things are used during the Sukkot holiday: Lulav, Etrog, _____, and _____.

הָאֶתְרוֹג וְהַלּוּלָב

WHAT is the proper way to recite the blessings on the Lulav and Etrog?

YOU HOLD the Lulav in your right hand and the Etrog in your left, both hands together. Now you recite the blessing by holding the Etrog upside down with its tip downward.

When the blessings are finished you reverse the Etrog, tip upwards. Now you wave your Lulav in all directions: east, south, west, north, upwards and downwards—
All this time the Lulav and Etrog are held together.

חַג שָׂמֵחַ!

WHAT is the proper greeting on Sukkot?

SUKKOT is a happy holiday. On Sukkot you say "Chag Sameach," "happy holiday." You can use the same greeting for Chanukah, Purim, Shavuot, Tu Bishvat, and Lag B'Omer.

If you wish, you can add the name of a holiday between two words. You can say "Chag Sukkot Sameach." You can use the same type of greeting for all happy holidays. All you have to do is insert the name of the holiday.

13

SIMCHAT TORAH שִׂמְחַת תּוֹרָה

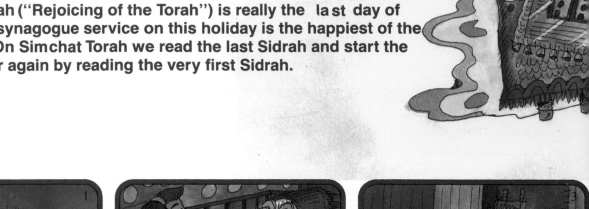

The Torah is our most precious possession. Each week in the synagogue we read a new Sidrah in the Torah. It takes exactly a whole year to read all the fifty-four Sidrot.

Simchat Torah ("Rejoicing of the Torah") is really the last day of Sukkot. The synagogue service on this holiday is the happiest of the whole year. On Simchat Torah we read the last Sidrah and start the Torah all over again by reading the very first Sidrah.

The person called to recite the blessings over the last Sidrah is called Chatan Torah ("Torah bridegroom").

Another person recites the blessings over the reading of the first Torah portion. This person is called Chatan Bereshit ("Starting bridegroom").

All the Torot are taken out of the Aron Kodesh. The members of the synagogue carry the Torot around the temple in a special parade called Hakafot.

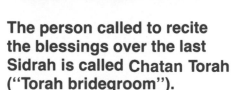

The Hakafot parade circles the synagogue seven times. Dancing and singing children and adults parade behind the Torot waving colorful Simchat Torah flags.

When the Torah reading and the Hakafot are over, the service is ended. On Simchat Torah we learn that the study of Torah has no end. It's great to be Jewish and have the Torah teach us to be good human beings.

YOUR HEBREW WORD LIST

שִׂמְחַת־תּוֹרָה	Simchat Torah	"Rejoicing of the Torah"
הַקָּפוֹת	Hakafot	Processions with the Torah
סִדְרָה	Sidrah	Torah portion of the week
דֶּגֶל, דְּגָלִים	Degel	Flag
אֲרוֹן קוֹדֶשׁ	Aron Kodesh	Holy Ark

CHOOSE YOUR ANSWER FROM THE WORD LIST
Write your answer in English or in Hebrew.

1. On the holiday of _____ we read the last and first chapters of the Torah.

2. The _____ parade circles the synagogue seven times.

3. On Simchat Torah we read the last_____ and the first _____ of the Torah.

4. The Torot are kept in a specially decorated ark called _____ _____.

5. The Hakafot parade includes children and adults waving specially designed Simchat Torah_____.

הַתּוֹרָה

WHY did God give the Torah to the Jews?

BECAUSE God first offered the Torah to other nations and they refused it.

Before giving the Torah to the Israelites, God offered it to various other nations of the world. "Will you accept and obey My Torah?" God asked the first nation.

"What does it say?" they asked.

"It says, 'You shall not kill,'" answered God.

"We cannot accept and obey the Torah," answered the first nation. "Throughout our history we have lived by the sword."

Then God asked the second nation, "Will you accept and obey My Torah?"

"What does it say?" they asked.

"It says 'Honor your father and your mother,'" answered God.

"We cannot accept and obey the Torah," answered the second nation. "We reject our parents when they grow old."

God asked all the nations of the world. But none would promise to accept and obey the Torah. Then God asked Israel. The Israelites did not ask what was in the Torah. They did not hesitate. They answered, "All that God has spoken we will do and we will obey."

CHANUKAH חֲנֻכָּה

Chanukah is a story of heroes and heroines, who fought a war for freedom and liberty.

The story of Chanukah goes back thousands of years. At that time the land of Israel was ruled by a cruel Syrian king named Antiochus.

He tried to destroy the Jewish people by forcing them to pray to wooden and stone idols.

One day a troop of Syrian soldiers came to the town of Modin and tried to force the people there to worship an idol.

Instead of bowing down, the priest Mattathias killed the Syrian officer and fled to the mountains of Judah.

Mattathias and his five sons organized an army to fight the Syrians. Under the leadership of Judah Maccabee, the Jews defeated the Syrians and recaptured Jerusalem and the Holy Temple.

After much work, the Maccabeans rebuilt the whole Temple.

When the Temple was ready, all they could find was one tiny jar of holy oil for the Menorah. A miracle happened, and this tiny jar of oil kept the Menorah alight for eight whole days. Because of this miracle we celebrate the holiday of Chanukah for eight days.

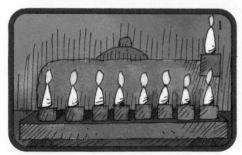

In memory of the miracle of Chanukah we light the Chanukiah for eight days. The first night we light one candle, and every other night we light one more candle until all eight are alight.

Chanukah is draydel-playing time. Each of the four Hebrew letters on the draydel stands for a Hebrew word. Nun, Gimel, Hay, and Shin stand for *Ness Gadol Hayah Shom,* "A great miracle happened there."

Antiochus did not allow the Jews to study Torah. The Jews fooled the Syrians by making believe they were playing draydel instead of studying Torah.

A favorite Chanukah food is latkes. A latke is a potato pancake that is fried until it is crispy and crunchy. In Hebrew latkes are called *l'veevot.*

Long ago it was a custom to give a coin to each child after the candles were lit. These coins were called, in Yiddish, "Chanukah Gelt." Today parents also give Chanukah Gelt to their children.

Chanukah starts on the 25th day of the month Kislev. Chanukah is a happy time for everyone. To make Chanukah even happier in some homes, children receive a gift for each night of Chanukah—eight nights, eight gifts.

YOUR HEBREW WORD LIST

חֲנֻכָּה	Chanukah	Dedication
סְבִיבוֹן	S'veevon	Spinning top (draydel in Yiddish)
לְבִיבוֹת	L'veevot	Potato pancakes (latkes in Yiddish)
חֲנֻכִּיָּה	Chanukiah	Chanukah menorah
נֵס גָּדוֹל הָיָה שָׁם	Nes Gadol Hayah Shom	"A great miracle happened there"

CHOOSE YOUR ANSWER FROM THE WORD LIST
Write your answer in English or in Hebrew.

1. The Menorah used on Chanukah is
   called a _____.

2. A _____ has four sides and spins round and
   round.

3. The four Hebrew letters on the draydel stand for the
   Hebrew phrase _____.

4. Because of the miracle of the tiny jar of oil which burned for
   eight days, we celebrate the holiday of _____.

5. _____ are delicious fried, crispy potato pancakes.

הַדְלָקַת הַנֵּרוֹת לַחֲנֻכָּה

WHAT is the correct way to light the Chanukiah?

OUR RABBIS say that you place the first candle on the right side of the Chanukiah. The second candle is placed next to it, and so on, always moving to the left. Now you light the Shammos candle and recite the Chanukah blessings. You light the candles, always starting from the left and moving towards the right.

As you light the candles you recite or sing the hymn Hanerot Hallalu. This is followed by the song Maoz Tzur.

It is important that everyone be aware that the celebration of Chanukah is taking place. You therefore place the Chanukiah in a spot where it can be visible from outside the home.

WHAT is the proper greeting on Chanukah?

ON CHANUKAH you greet acquaintances by saying, "Chag, Chanukah Sameach." If you wish to greet someone in Yiddish you say, "Ah freylachin Chanukah." This means, "A Happy Chanukah."

TU BISHVAT ט״ו בִּשְׁבָט

Trees are very important to the health of the world. Half of the animals and birds in this world live in forests. Trees provide us with fruits to eat and lumber for our homes. Would you be surprised to learn that many medicines come from trees? The roots of trees prevent landslides. Trees also keep the air clean and healthy. Without trees the ozone layer would disappear, and our planet could burn up.

The Torah knew the importance of trees. Jews were warned not to destroy trees even during a war. "You may eat of them, but you must not cut them down."

We Jews have a special holiday to honor the trees. This special day is called Rosh Hashanah La-ilanot—New Year of the Trees. The holiday of trees is on Tu Bishvat.

The word "Tu" is made up of two Hebrew letters, Tet and Vav. Tet has a numeral value of 9, and Vav has a value of 6. Added together they equal 15. The holiday of Tu Bishvat is on the fifteenth day of the month of Shevat.

In ancient Israel, parents would plant a tree when a child was born. When two young people married, branches were cut from their trees. These branches were used to support their Chuppah—the canopy under which the wedding ceremony takes place.

The rainy season is over, and the time is just right for tree planting. Israeli children leave their classrooms and march into the rocky fields with shovels and tiny trees. They sing and dance as they plant their trees.

The Jewish National Fund, since 1880, has planted millions of trees in Israel. Now, because of the JNF, the hills and valleys are carpeted with green trees.

You can also plant trees in Israel. You can contribute money to the JNF, who will plant trees for you.

You also show our love for Israel and Tu Bi Shvat by eating fruits from Israel on this day. Israeli fruits are dates, figs, raisins, and a special fruit called bokser. Bokser is the dried fruit of a carob tree.

YOUR HEBREW WORD LIST

ט"ו בִּשְׁבָט	Tu Bishvat	Fifteenth of month of Shevat
רֹאשׁ הַשָׁנָה לָאִילָנוֹת	Rosh Hashanah La-ilanot	New Year of the Trees
חָרוּב	Charuv	Carob tree (bokser in Yiddish)
שְׁבָט	Shevat	A month in the Jewish year
פֵּרוֹת	Perot	Fruits

CHOOSE YOUR ANSWER FROM THE WORD LIST
Write your answer in English or in Hebrew.

1. The Holiday of Trees is celebrated on _____.
2. Bokser is the Yiddish word for _____.
3. _____ is a month in the Jewish year.
4. On Tu Bishvat we eat _____ from Israel.
5. The holiday of _____ is on the 15th day of the month Shevat.

HEBREW SPY CODE.
Substitute English letters for the Hebrew and you will decipher the secret message.

חט ראי ‏ יחט ‏ סיירט טסךחטעף

פם ‏ נרמב ‏ דלמסךף

A	א
B	ב
C	ה
D	ד
E	י
F	שׁ
G	ג
H	ה
I	ח
J	ת
K	כ
L	ל
M	מ
N	נ
O	ר
P	פ
Q	ק
R	ס
S	ט
T	ס
U	ו
V	ף
W	ז
X	י
Y	ץ
Z	צ

19

PURIM פּוּרִים

The noisiest and zaniest holiday of the Jewish year is Purim. The story of Purim is found in the Bible scroll called Megillat Esther.

Thousands of years ago there were many Jews in the kingdom of Persia. Ahasuerus, the king of Persia, held a beauty contest. A Jewish woman named Esther won the contest and became his queen.

Sometime later, Esther's uncle, Mordecai, overheard a Persian, called Haman, plotting to kill all the Jews in Persia. Mordecai asked Esther, the queen, to go to King Ahasuerus and save the Jews of Persia.

Brave Queen Esther put her life in danger and appeared before the king. Ahasuerus asked Esther, "Who is this evil person who wishes to harm you and your people?"

Esther replied and pointed to Haman, "It is wicked Haman. He built a gallows on which to hang my Uncle Mordecai."

"Then let Haman be hanged on the gallows which he has built for Mordecai," commanded the king.

Haman was hanged and the Jews of Persia were saved.

Purim is observed in the synagogue by reading the Scroll of Esther. Every time Haman's name is read, everybody boos and makes lots of noise.

All the children have special noisemakers called ra-ashanim. In Yiddish they are called graggers. The idea of making noise is to erase the name of evil Haman.

After the Purim service there is a party and a masquerade. Kids and adults dress up in all kinds of funny costumes and masks.

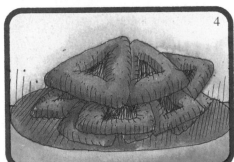

On Purim we eat Hamantashen. This is a delicious three-cornered cake filled with jam or poppy seeds.

The three-cornered cake is said to be just like Haman's ears. In Hebrew. Hamantashen are called Ozney Haman—Haman's ears.

The most delightful Purim custom is the sending of Shalach Manot (Purim gifts). On this happy holiday you send and receive baskets of goodies filled with Hamantashen and other delicious foods.

20

YOUR HEBREW WORD LIST

מְגִלָּה	Megillah	A scroll (book of the Bible)
רַעֲשָׁנִים	Ra-ashanim	Noisemaker (gragger in Yiddish)
שָׁלַח מָנוֹת	Shalach Manot	Sending portions, gifts, candy
אָזְנֵי הָמָן	Oznay Haman	Purim cakes · Hamantashen
אֶסְתֵּר	Esther	Jewish queen who saved the Jews of Persia

CHOOSE YOUR ANSWER FROM THE WORD LIST
Write your answer in English or in Hebrew.

1. The story of Purim is found in the _____.

2. Every time Haman's name is mentioned you make lots of noise with your _____.

3. _____ are three-cornered cakes filled with jam or poppy seeds.

4. On Purim you get and send _____.

5. The queen of Persia was a Jewish girl named _____.

SYMBOL CODE
To decipher this code, substitute the letter for the indicated symbol.

A ☉	N ♌
B ♃	O ♏
C ♄	P ♎
D ♂	Q ♏
E ♅	R ⚹
F ☿	S ♈
G ♀	T ♓
H ♂	U ♈
I ☿	V ♒
J ☽	W ⟩
K ♃	X ⟫
L ‖	Y ⊓
M ♋	Z ⟨

START
_ _ _ _ _ _ _ _ _

_ _ _ _ _ _ _ _ _

מְגִלַּת אֶסְתֵּר

WHY do we read the Book of Esther on the holiday of Purim?

BECAUSE the Book of Esther contains the story of the miracle of Purim.

Even though God's name is not mentioned even once in the Megillah, it is obvious that without the Lord's help the Jews of Persia would have been killed.

Our sages say that even when God's helping is not seen, it is always present. Nothing happens by accident. Everything is part of God's master plan.

PASSOVER פֶּסַח

Thousands of years ago, the Hebrews were slaves in the land of Egypt. They worked very hard and built palaces and cities for the Egyptians. The cruel king of Egypt was called Pharaoh.

Moses and his brother Aaron went to the palace of Pharaoh. They said, "Let my people go free." The wicked Pharaoh refused to free the Hebrews.

So God sent ten terrible plagues over the land of Egypt. After the tenth plague, Pharaoh let the Hebrew people go free. The Hebrews left Egypt in a great hurry. They had no time to bake bread. So they placed the raw dough on their backs and marched out of Egypt. The hot desert sun baked the dough into Matzah. Then Pharaoh changed his mind. He sent the Egyptian army after the Hebrews. God saved them. The Egyptian soldiers were drowned in the Red Sea.

The holiday of Passover celebrates the freeing of the Hebrew slaves from Egypt. Passover begins on the 15th day of Nisan.

Passover starts with the Seder. Everyone at the Seder has a special prayer book called a Haggadah.

On the table is a Karah. The Karah holds five special foods.

On the table is a cup of wine is for Elijah the Prophet. We pray that Elijah will visit our Seder.

Nearby is a Matzah holder with three Matzot. On Passover you eat no bread. You eat only Matzah.

The Seder starts with the lighting of the candles and the singing of Kiddush.

The youngest child asks the four questions. In Hebrew we call the four questions "Arba Kushiyot."

The leader hides a piece of matzah called "Afikomen." Someone steals the Afikomen. The finder gets a special gift.

We end the Seder by singing "L'Shanah Habah B'Yerushali m"— "Next year in Jerusalem."

YOUR HEBREW WORD LIST

פַּרְעֹה	Pharaoh	King of Egypt who enslaved the Hebrews
מֹשֶׁה	Moshe	Moses, the leader and prophet of Israel
פֶּסַח	Pesach	Passover
מִצְרַיִם	Mitzrayim	Egypt
אֲפִיקוֹמֶן	Afikomen	Greek word meaning "dessert"

CHOOSE YOUR ANSWER FROM THE WORD LIST
Write your answer in English or in Hebrew.

1. The cruel king of Egypt was called _____.

2. _____ was the Jewish leader who freed the Israelites from Egypt.

3. Whoever finds the _____ gets a special gift.

4. Pharaoh was the king of _____.

5. The holiday of _____ celebrates the freeing of the Hebrew slaves from Egypt.

SEMAPHORE CODE
To decipher this code substitute the letter for the semaphore signal.

START

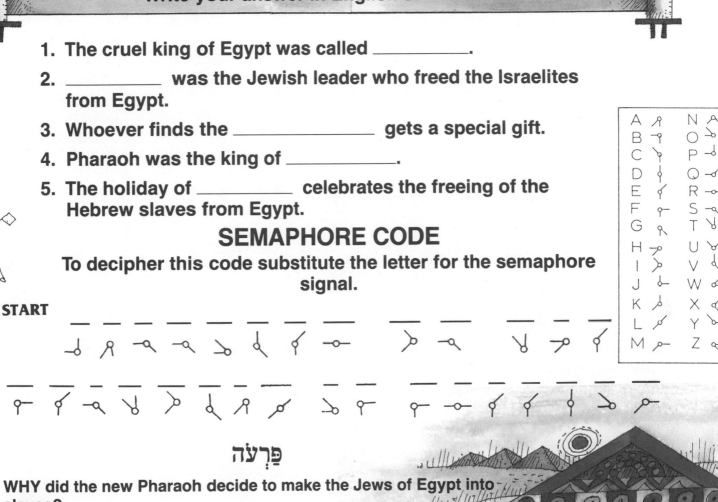

פַּרְעֹה

WHY did the new Pharaoh decide to make the Jews of Egypt into slaves?

BECAUSE the new Pharaoh was afraid of the Jews. The old Pharaoh remembered the good things that Joseph had done for Egypt. He also remembered that the Jews were good neighbors and very friendly people.

The new Pharaoh was prejudiced against the Jews.

The word "prejudice" means to dislike a person, a special group, a race of people, or a religion without any reason.

23

YOUR SEDER DICTIONARY מָלוֹן שֶׁל פֶּסַח

HAGGADAH
Haggadah means "telling." This prayerbook is read during the Seder ceremony. It contains prayers, and songs praising God for taking the Jews out of Egypt.

KARAH
A special plate with five Passover symbols. Each of these foods tell us something about the holiday of Passover. The five foods are Charoset, Karpas, Maror, Baytzah, and Z'roah.

CUP OF ELIJAH:
Towards the end of the Seder we open the door and welcome Elijah the Prophet into our home. Everyone at the Seder prays that Elijah will bring us a year of peace, health, and happiness.

MATZAH: The Jews in Egypt did not have time to bake bread before leaving. They took raw dough which the hot desert sun baked into Matzah. During the holiday of Passover we eat only Matzah.

KARPAS: Parsley is a green vegetable; it reminds us of the things that come to life each spring.

MAROR: These bitter herbs remind us of the slaves in Egypt.

BAYTZAH: The roasted egg is a symbol of life.

Z'ROAH: This roasted shankbone reminds us of the lambs the Jews brought to the Holy Temple on Passover.

CHAROSET: It looks like cement and reminds us of slavery in Egypt.

SALT WATER: The bitter taste reminds us of the salty tears and the suffering of our ancestors in Egypt.

FOUR CUPS OF WINE: At the Seder you drink four cups of wine. Each cup represents one of God's promises to free the Israelites from slavery.

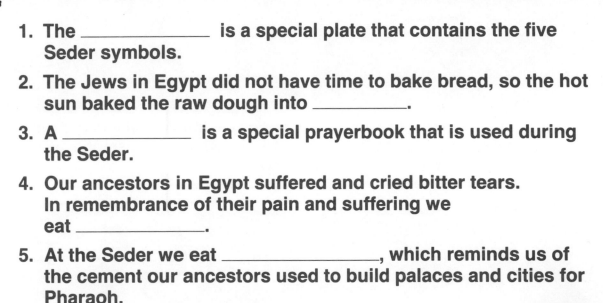

YOUR HEBREW WORD LIST

קְעָרָה	Karah	Compartmented Seder plate
מַצָּה	Matzah	Unleavened bread
חֲרוֹסֶת	Charoset	Mixture of chopped apples, nuts, wine, and cinnamon
מָרוֹר	Maror	Bitter herbs
הַגָּדָה	Haggadah	"The telling" (of the Pesach story)

CHOOSE YOUR ANSWER FROM THE WORD LIST
Write your answer in English or in Hebrew.

1. The _____ is a special plate that contains the five Seder symbols.

2. The Jews in Egypt did not have time to bake bread, so the hot sun baked the raw dough into _____.

3. A _____ is a special prayerbook that is used during the Seder.

4. Our ancestors in Egypt suffered and cried bitter tears. In remembrance of their pain and suffering we eat _____.

5. At the Seder we eat _____, which reminds us of the cement our ancestors used to build palaces and cities for Pharaoh.

מָעוֹת חִטִּים

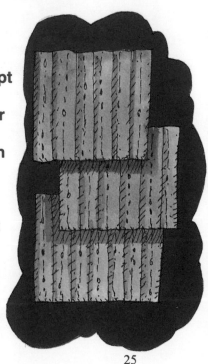

WHY do we give Tzedakah before Passover?

BECAUSE Passover reminds us of the suffering of our people in Egypt long ago.

Tzedakah means "charity." We do Tzedakah when we help the poor and those who cannot help themselves.

Right after the holiday of Purim, the synagogues and temples begin collecting Tzedakah for the holiday of Pesach.

This special Tzedakah money is called Maot Chittim ("money for wheat").

Years ago Maot Chittim money was used to buy wheat. This wheat was baked into matzah for poor people.

It is a mitzvah to share with others and to help them. Helping and sharing is something God wants us to do. If we share with other people, we are helping make the world a better place in which to live.

Sometimes, we do not know any people to help. Synagogues and temples collect the Maot Chittim money and buy food, clothing, and medicine for people who need it.

YOM HASHOAH (Holocaust Day) יוֹם הַשּׁוֹאָה

Yom Hashoah is a new holiday. It is one of the sad times on the Jewish calendar.

The Hebrew word *shoah* means "Holocaust." It describes the most horrible event that ever happened in the world and in Jewish history.

In 1933 Adolf Hitler, a madman, became the chancellor of Germany. Under his leadership the Nazis killed more than six million Jews. Innocent men, women, and children were beaten, tortured, and killed in concentration and death camps.

On the seventh day of the month of Nisan we remember those who were victims of the Nazis. Synagogues observe Yom HaShoah (Holocaust Day) with a special service.

Candles are lit by survivors and children of survivors. After that, memorial prayers are recited.

In Israel a ceremony takes place at Yad Vashem in Jerusalem. Yad Vashem is the memorial center for the Holocaust.

Israeli radio and TV stations broadcast prayers and programs about the Holocaust all day long. During the day, at a special time, everyone and everything stops to observe a moment of silence.

People all over the world, Jews and non-Jews, pray that never again will there be a Holocaust to anyone, anywhere.

YOUR HEBREW WORD LIST

שׁוֹאָה	Shoah	The Holocaust
יוֹם הַשׁוֹאָה	Yom HaShoah	Holocaust Memorial Day
נִיסָן	Nisan	A month in the Jewish year.
יָד־וָשֵׁם	Yad Vashem	Holocaust Memorial Center in Jerusalem

CHOOSE YOUR ANSWER FROM THE WORD LIST
Write your answer in English or in Hebrew.

1. The word _____ means "Holocaust."

2. Holocaust Memorial Day is _____.

3. Yom HaShoah falls on the seventh day of the month of _____.

4. The _____ in Jerusalem is the memorial center for the Holocaust.

DIAL-A-MESSAGE
The first number tells you what circle to look at. The second number tells you which letter to write down. For example: 7-1 is "P" (the first letter on the "7" circle).

START

___ ___ ___   ___ ___ ___ ___ ___ ___ ___
9-3 6-3 6-1   4-2 2-1 7-3 4-2 6-3 2-1 4-2

___ ___   ___   ___ ___ ___   ___ ___ ___
4-3 7-3   2-1   7-3 2-1 3-1   3-1 2-1 9-3

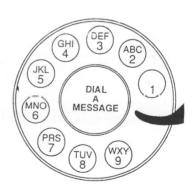

YOM HA'ATZMAUT יוֹם הָעַצְמָאוּת

The Torah says that God talked to Moses and said, "My people must be taken out of Egypt! Go. Lead them to the land of Canaan, where there is milk and honey."

The ancient land of Canaan is the modern State of Israel. In the last 2,000 years many nations have taken turns ruling Israel. The Persians, the Arabs, the Turks, and last of all the British. But no matter who ruled, there were always Jews living in Israel. They dreamed of a miracle. They dreamed of a Jewish state.

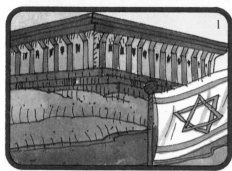

One of the most glorious days in the long history of the Jews came on the fifth of Iyar, which in the year 1948 came out on May 14th. After centuries of struggle, Israel once again became a Jewish state.
Every year, Jews all over the world celebrate the creation of the modern State of Israel.

Yom Ha'Atzmaut is the Hebrew name for Israel Independence Day. It is celebrated out in the open with singing and dancing. There is a giant parade with lots of fireworks. It is as if all of Israel is having one big birthday party. Happy Birthday, Israel!

In synagogues all around the world, special prayers in honor of Independence Day are added to the daily service. Jews everywhere celebrate the great day on the fifth of Iyar each year.

This is the flag of the State of Israel. It is blue and white. There is a six-pointed star in the center.

Here is the emblem of the State of Israel. The Temple Menorah is surrounded by green olive branches.

Every country has a national anthem. The Israeli anthem is called Hatikvah, "The Hope."

Jerusalem is the capital of Israel. The Western Wall is in Jerusalem. The Western Wall was a part of the wall around the Second Temple.

YOUR HEBREW WORD LIST

יוֹם הָעַצְמָאוּת	Yom Ha'Atzmaut	Israel Independence Day
הַתִּקְוָה	Hatikvah	"The Hope" (Israel national anthem)
אִייָר	Iyar	A month in the Jewish year.
כּוֹתֶל־הַמַּעֲרָבִי	Kotel Hamaravi	Western Wall, the last remnant of the Holy Temple in Jerusalem
דֶּגֶל	Degel	Flag

CHOOSE YOUR ANSWER FROM THE WORD LIST

Write your answer in English or in Hebrew.

1. The holiday of Yom Ha'Atzmaut falls on the fifth day of the month of _____.

2. The _____ was a part of the Second Temple.

3. _____ is the national anthem of the State of Israel.

4. The _____ of Israel has a six-pointed star in the center.

5. _____ is Israel Independence Day.

FIND THE WORD
Unscramble these two story words.

יוֹם הַזִּכָּרוֹן

WHAT is the name of the Israeli holiday before Yom Ha'Atzmaut?

IN ISRAEL, the day before Yom Ha'Atzmaut is called Yom HaZikaron. Yom means "day," HaZikaron means "remembrance."

On this day the Israelis remember their children, the heroes and heroines who died defending Israel against Arab attacks.

29

LAG B'OMER לַ"ג בָּעֹמֶר

The Jews in ancient Israel were excellent farmers, but their crops depended upon the sun and the rain. If there was little rain there was a poor harvest, and thousands of people could die of hunger. Harvest time for the wheat and barley crop was the period between Passover and Shavuot. At this serious period of time, the Jewish farmers prayed for good weather so they could harvest their crops and feed their families.

Each day, right after Passover, the Kohen in the Holy Temple measured out a quantity of grain called an Omer. The Kohen would recite special prayers over the grain and pray for a good and bountiful harvest. This Omer ceremony was performed for the 49 days between Passover and Shavuot. These 49 days are called Sefirot HaOmer, the counting of the Omer.

On the 33rd day of the counting of the Omer, we celebrate the holiday of Lag B'Omer. The Hebrew word Lag is made up of the letters Lamed and Gimel. In Hebrew the Lamed has a numberical value of 30, and the Gimel has a value of 3. Add these two together and you will get 33. Lag B'Omer means "33 days into the counting of the Omer."

The Sefirah was a sacred and serious time. A good harvest meant life. A drought or insects meant death and starvation. During the Sefirah days there were no weddings and celebrations except on Lag B'Omer and Rosh Hodesh.

But on the 33rd day, our sadness turns to joy. Lag B'Omer becomes a day of picnics, and bow-and-arrow contests. And lots of good picnic food.
Why is Lag B'Omer a happy time while all the other days in the Omer are sad?

About 2,000 years ago the Romans ruled the land of Israel. The Romans refused to allow the Jews to study Torah and pray to their God. Rabbi Akiba was a great leader and a Torah scholar. To fool the Romans, the Torah students carried bows and arrows and pretended they were hunting.

Bar Kochba ("Son of a Star") led a revolt against the Romans. Bar Kochba and his Torah soldiers won many battles, and on Lag B'Omer they captured the city of Jerusalem.
The powerful Romans surrounded Bar Kochba and his Torah soldiers in the city of Betar. In the end, on Tisha B'Av (the ninth of Av), Bar Kochba and his soldiers died defending Betar.

YOUR HEBREW WORD LIST

לַ״ג בָּעוֹמֶר	Lag B'Omer	Thirty-third day of the counting of the Omer
עוֹמֶר	Omer	Sheaf, measure
סְפִירָה	Sefirah	Time of Counting the Omer
בַּר־כּוֹכְבָא	Bar Kochba	Leader of the Jewish revolt against Rome (132–135 C.E.)
רַבִּי עֲקִיבָא	Rabbi Akiba	Great Jewish teacher

CHOOSE YOUR ANSWER FROM THE WORD LIST
Write your answer in English or in Hebrew.

1. A _____ was a measure of grain.

2. The 49 days between Passover and Shavuot are called _____.

3. _____ was the leader of the Jewish revolt against the Roman rule.

4. _____ was a Torah scholar and a great Jewish leader.

5. The holiday that is celebrated on the 33rd day of the counting of the Omer is called _____.

MYSTERY MESSAGE

START

Use the code and find the message.

S	K	A
F	H	D
T	N	O

I	B	L
C	R	M
Y	E	W

_ _ _ _ _   _ _ _ _ _ _   _ _ _

_ _   _ _ _ _ _   _ _ _ _

רַב שִׁמְעוֹן בַּר יוֹחַאי

WHO was Rabbi Shimon bar Yohai?

In Israel, Lag B'Omer is also observed as the birthday of Rabbi Shimon bar Yohai, the author of the mystical book Zohar. Great numbers of people visit the rabbi's grave in the city of Meron. There is much singing and dancing around a huge bonfire. Around the bonfire stories are told about Bar Kochba, Rabbi Akiba, and Shimon bar Yohai—heroes who kept the flames of liberty and Torah Judaism alive.

SHAVUOT שָׁבוּעוֹת

Moses led the Hebrews out of Egypt. After several weeks of marching through the hot desert, they came to Mount Sinai. Moses climbed to the top of the mountain.

The Torah says, "There was thunder and lightening. A thick cloud covered the mountain. The sound of a shofar echoed through the air. The whole mountain shook. Then God gave Moses and the Hebrews the Ten Commandments."

The holiday of Shavuot celebrates the giving of the Ten Commandments (Aseret Hadibrot) on Mount Sinai.

Shavuot means "weeks." The holiday of Shavuot is celebrated seven weeks after Passover on the 15th day of Sivan.

Shavuot is the time of the barley harvest in Israel. Shavuot also celebrates the harvest of the first fruits in Israel.

In ancient Israel the farmers bought the first fruits, or Bikkurim, to the Holy Temple in Jerusalem.

Today we celebrate Shavuot by going to the synagogue and reading special prayers.

At home we celebrate Shavuot by decorating the house with flowers and green plants.

On Shavuot we eat special foods that are made with milk and cheese. Dishes such as blintzes and cheese pies are favorite treats.

In some synagogues there is a Bikkurim ceremony. We decorate the synagogue with baskets of fruits and flowers. This ceremony reminds us of the Bikkurim in ancient Israel.

YOUR HEBREW WORD LIST

שָׁבוּעוֹת	Shavuot	Weeks
קָצִיר	Katzir	Harvest
עֲשֶׂרֶת הַדִּבְּרוֹת	Aseret Hadibrot	Ten Commandments
בִּכּוּרִים	Bikkurim	First Fruits
מֹשֶׁה	Moshe	Moses, the leader and prophet of Israel

CHOOSE YOUR ANSWER FROM THE WORD LIST
Write your answer in English or in Hebrew.

1. The holiday of _____ starts on the 6th day of Sivan.

2. In ancient Israel the farmers brought _____ to the Temple.

3. God gave Moses the _____ on Mount Sinai.

4. Shavuot was the time of the barley _____ in Israel.

5. _____ led the Israelites out of Egypt.

HEBREW SPY CODE.
Substitute English letters for the Hebrew and you will decipher the secret message.

START

____ ____ ____ ____

ע   א מ   ט ח י   ד ך ר ל

____ ____

ץ ד ם ר   ג ד ד

מְגִלַּת רוּת

A	א
B	ב
C	
D	ג
E	ד
F	ה
G	ו
H	ז
I	ח
J	ט
K	י
L	כ
M	ל
N	מ
O	נ
P	ס
Q	ע
R	פ
S	צ
T	ק
U	ר
V	ש
W	ת
X	
Y	
Z	צ

WHY do we read the Book of Ruth on the holiday of Shavuot?
BECAUSE of three reasons:
1. Shavuot is also called the "Harvest Festival," and the story of Ruth and Boaz took place at harvest-time.
2. King David was the great-grandson of Ruth and Boaz. According to tradition, King David died on Shavuot.
3. Ruth was a convert to Judaism. The story of how she accepted the Jewish religion is well-suited to Shavuot, the holiday commemorating the acceptance of the Torah by Israel.

THE TEN COMMANDMENTS עֲשֶׂרֶת הַדִּבְּרוֹת

The Ten Commandments, which God gave Moses, are more important than any laws ever made by one person or by any country. These laws were first carved on tablets of stone. Fathers and mothers taught them to their children. The children then taught the laws to other families.

Today, people all over the world live by the Ten Commandments God gave Moses.

Let's talk about four of these commandments:

1. I am the Lord, your God: Sometimes we forget that God created the world and everything in it. It is important to obey God's commandments and to give thanks for the wonderful gift of life.

4. Remember the Sabbath and keep it holy: On one day each week, on the Sabbath, Jews stop the long week of work and turn their thoughts to God. You go to temple, sing songs of praise, and thank God for the wonderful world and your loving family.

5. Honor your father and your mother: God gave you parents to love and who take care of you until you are grown up enough to take care of yourself. They want only what is best for you. You honor your parents by listening, obeying, and helping the family work as a team.

10. You shall not want what is your neighbor's." Sometimes boys and girls want things that other children have. They want them so badly that they become very unhappy if they do not get them. Many times, when we get something we think we want, we find out that it does not make us happy at all. We only wanted it because somebody else had it.

Name the other six commandments and talk about them.

אָנֹכִי ה׳ אֱלֹהֶיךָ

The Midrash says that when God gave the Aseret Hadibrot to Israel, the whole world was quiet. No birds sang or flew. No lion roared, no angels flew, the seas were calm and no creature spoke, and God said "Ani Adonai Elohim"—"I am Adonai your God."

The divine voice spoke in all languages, so that everyone in the world could understand the Commandments.

On Shavuot the Torah portion containing the Aseret Hadibrot is read. In some synagogues it is customary for the congregants to stand and to repeat the Ten Commandments with the Torah reader. Read the Commandments in English or in Hebrew.

א. אָנֹכִי ה׳ אֱלֹהֶיךָ	"I am Adonai your God."
ב. לֹא־יִהְיֶה לְךָ אֱלֹהִים אֲחֵרִים עַל־פָּנָי	You shall have no other gods before Me!
ג. לֹא תִשָּׂא אֶת־שֵׁם ה׳ אֱלֹהֶיךָ לַשָּׁוְא	You shall not take the name of God in vain.
ד. זָכוֹר אֶת־יוֹם הַשַּׁבָּת לְקַדְּשׁוֹ	Remember Shabbat and keep it holy.
ה. כַּבֵּד אֶת־אָבִיךָ וְאֶת־אִמֶּךָ	Honor your father and your mother.
ו. לֹא תִּרְצָח	You shall not kill.
ז. לֹא תִּנְאָף	You shall not be unfaithful to wife or husband.
ח. לֹא תִּגְנֹב	You shall not steal.
ט. לֹא־תַעֲנֶה בְרֵעֲךָ עֵד שָׁקֶר	You shall not bear false witness.
י. לֹא תַחְמֹד בֵּית רֵעֶךָ	

CHOOSE YOUR ANSWER

Check the four commandments on page 34.

1. I am _____ your God.

2. Remember the _____ and keep it holy.

3. _____ Your father and your mother.

4. You shall not_____.

Name the other six commandments and talk about them.

SHALOSH REGALIM שָׁלֹשׁ רְגָלִים

Passover, Shavuot, and Sukkot are called the three Pilgrimage Festivals. A pilgrimage is a trip to a holy place. In ancient Israel the holy place was the Temple in Jerusalem.

The Hebrew word *shalosh* means "three." The Hebrew word *regel* means "foot." Shalosh Regalim means "three festival days when you march on foot."

Three times a year, the farmers of Israel brought the best of their fruits to the Holy Temple in Jerusalem. From the four corners of Israel, with song and dance, the people marched to the Holy Temple. At the city gate they were met by Levites who marched with them to the accompaniment of harps, drums and horns.

On Sukkot the farmers brought the best of their autumn crops to the Holy Temple. They marched to Jerusalem carrying palm branches and etrogim. In Jerusalem they lived in sukkot just as their ancestors did.

Today we celebrate by building sukkot, by reciting the blessings over the lulav and etrog, and going to Temple.

On Passover the farmers brought the best of the wheat harvest.

Today we celebrate Passover by eating matzot, going to the synagogue, and holding a Seder.

On Shavuot the farmers brought the best of the barley and fruit harvest.

Today we celebrate Shavuot by going to the synagogue, reading the Ten Commandments and eating cheese dishes.

YOUR HEBREW WORD LIST

שָׁלֹשׁ רְגָלִים	Shalosh Regalim	Pilgrimage Festivals
בֵּית־הַמִּקְדָּשׁ	Bet Hamikdash	The Holy Temple
פֶּסַח	Pesach	Passover
שָׁבוּעוֹת	Shavuot	Weeks
סֻכּוֹת	Sukkot	Festival of Booths

CHOOSE YOUR ANSWER FROM THE WORD LIST
Write your answer in English or in Hebrew.

1. On _____ the Jewish farmers marched to Jerusalem carrying palm branches and etrogim.

2. Today we celebrate _____ by eating matzah and going to a Seder.

3. On the holiday of _____ we read the Ten Commandments.

4. In Hebrew we call the pilgrimage festivals
   _____.

5. Three times a year the Israelite farmers brought the best of their fruits to the _____.

SYMBOL CODE
To decipher this code, substitute the letter for the indicated symbol.

A ☉	N ♌
B ♃	O ♍
C ♄	P ♎
D ♅	Q ♏
E ♆	R ♐
F ♇	S ♑
G ♀	T ♒
H ♂	U ♓
I ☿	V ♒
J ☽	W >
K ☊	X ≫
L ‖	Y ⚹
M ♋	Z <

TISHA B'AV תִּשְׁעָה בְּאָב

The holiday of Tisha B'Av is the saddest time on the Jewish calendar. The word *tisha* means "nine," and Av is the ninth month of the Jewish year. Many sad things happened on the ninth day of Av. Four of the saddest are: the destruction of the First and Second Temples, the defeat of Bar Kochba, and the expulsion of Jews from Spain. On this day of mourning we also remember the six million Jews who were murdered by the Nazis.

For us Tisha B'Av is a day of fasting and mourning. The synagogue is lighted only by the glow of the Ner Tamid and the memorial bulbs.

The service is sad and tearful as we remember the terrible things that happened to the Jewish people. In some synagogues people sit on the floor and wear slippers or sneakers as a sign of mourning. At services a special book of the Bible is chanted. The Hebrew name of this book is Aycha. In English it is called "Lamentations." Remembering these sad times in Jewish history makes us work harder for a better world in which all people can live in peace and happiness.

Nebuchadnezzer, king of the Babylonians, sent an army to defeat the kingdom of Judah. His army of chariots, battering rams, and stone throwers defeated the Jews.

In 586 B.C.E., on the ninth day of Av, the Babylonians captured Jerusalem. They destroyed the Holy Temple.

Years later, the Jews returned to Israel. Once again they rebuilt the Holy Temple. Six hundred years later, in 70 C.E., on the ninth of Av, the second Holy Temple was destroyed.

Emperor Titus celebrated the victory by building an arch to celebrate his victory. This Arch of Titus can still be seen in Rome.

For sixty years, there was peace in Judea. The peace and quiet ended when the Roman Emperor Hadrian made it hard for the Jews to practice their religion.

Bar Kochba ("Son of a Star") rebelled against the Romans. His Jewish army recaptured Jerusalem. Freedom was won. For a moment.

After much fighting, the Romans surrounded Bar Kochba in the village of Betar. He and his Torah warriors died defending the Jewish people.

YOUR HEBREW WORD LIST

תִּשְׁעָה בְּאָב	Tisha B'Av	Ninth day of the month of Av
אָב	Av	A month in the Jewish year.
תִּשְׁעָה	Tisha	Nine
בַּר־כּוֹכְבָא	Bar Kochba	Leader of the revolt against Rome
יְרוּשָׁלַיִם	Yerushalayim	Jerusalem

CHOOSE YOUR ANSWER FROM THE WORD LIST
Write your answer in English or in Hebrew.

1. The Babylonians captured the city of _____ on Tisha B'Av.

2. The Hebrew word _____ means "nine."

3. The name _____ means "Son of a Star."

4. The holiday of _____ reminds us of the Jews who were driven out of Spain.

DIAL-A-MESSAGE
The first number tells you what circle to look at. The second number tells you which letter to write down. For example: 7-1 is "P" (the first letter on the "7" circle).

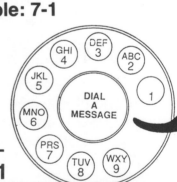

START

__ __ __   __ __ __ __ __ __
2-2 2-1 7-2   5-2 6-3 2-3 4-2 2-2 2-1

__ __ __ __ __   __ __ __   __ __   __
6-1 3-2 2-1 6-2 7-3   7-3 6-3 6-2   6-3 3-3   2-1

__ __ __ __
7-3 8-1 2-1 7-2

מְגִלַת אֵיכָה

WHY do we read the Book of Aycha during Tisha B'Av?

BECAUSE the scroll of Aycha is a very sad book. Some believe that the Prophet Jeremiah, who witnessed the destruction of Jerusalem, wrote the Scroll of Aycha.

Aycha is the third of the five Megillot in the Tanach.

39

SYNAGOGUE בֵּית־הַכְּנֶסֶת

"Synagogue" is a Greek word meaning "assembly" or "congregation." The Yiddish word is "shul."

Most holidays and life-cycle events relate in some way to the synagogue. The first synagogue was established by our exiled ancestors in Babylon about 586 B.C.E. They remembered Temple ceremonies when the priests recited passages from the Torah and Prophets. Our ancestors yearned for the holidays and feasts they practiced in ancient Israel. So they established a synagogue to serve their religious needs.

As America developed and the Jewish population grew, American Jewry divided into four different branches. Each branch of Judaism had different ideas of how to pray and what Jewish laws to observe. The four main branches are: Orthodox, Conservative, Reform, and Reconstructionist.

Synagogues are busy places and need many professional and educated people to serve the congregation and the school.

The rabbi is the leader of the congregation. He or she directs the services, gives sermons, and takes care of the school. The rabbi also helps people with their family problems. The word "rabbi" means "my teacher."

The Chazan, or cantor, assists the rabbi in leading the congregation in prayer. He or she sings the prayers and has an excellent musical voice. The cantor also teaches the Bar and Bat Mitzvah class.

The gabbai assists the rabbi and the cantor in the synagogue. The gabbai helps with the aliyot and the seating of the synagogue.

The principal, called m'nahel or m'nahelet in Hebrew, depending on whether male or female, is in charge of Jewish education in the synagogue.

YOUR HEBREW WORD LIST

חַזָּן	Chazan	Cantor
רַבִּי	Rabbi	Scholar, teacher
בֵּית־כְּנֶסֶת	Bet Knesset	Synagogue or temple
גַּבַּאי	Gabai	The person who assists the rabbi and the cantor during the services.
מְנַהֵל	M'nahel (m)	Principal of a religious school.
מְנַהֶלֶת	M'nahelet (f)	

CHOOSE YOUR ANSWER FROM THE WORD LIST
Write your answer in English or in Hebrew.

1. The _____ chants the prayers in the Bet Knesset.

2. The word _____ means "my teacher." He or she leads the congregation in prayer or study.

3. A _____ is a house of prayer. You hold meetings and discussions there.

4. _____ is the _____ in charge of
   (name)
   Jewish Education in our synagogue.

5. The _____ helps the rabbi and cantor during the services.

בֵּית־הַכְּנֶסֶת

The synagogue has several Hebrew names that help tell us about its function:

בֵּית־כְּנֶסֶת	Bet Knesset—a house of gathering.	You hold meetings and discussions there.
בֵּית־תְּפִלָּה	Bet Tefillah—a house of prayer.	You hold services and observe holidays there.
בֵּית־מִדְרָשׁ	Bet Midrash—a house of learning.	A school and library for young and old.

There are also many people who cheerfully volunteer their time and services for the good of the Jewish community. Some of them may be your parents, friends, or neighbors,

Who is the president of your synagogue?

Who is the president of the sisterhood?

Who is the president of the men's club?

Who is in charge of raising money for Tzedakah?

41

THE SIDDUR סִדּוּר

Prayers go back to the beginning of the world. Noah prayed to God when he was saved from the Flood. Sarah, Rebecca, Leah and Rachel, Abraham, Isaac and Jacob all prayed to God. The Jews in Egypt also prayed to God to save them from slavery.

Some of the prayers they recited are exactly like the prayers in our Siddur. Before that time there was no special prayerbook. Rabbis and poets composed their own prayers and then memorized them.

In olden days there were no prayerbooks. Instead, a leader, a prophet, or a rabbi would lead the people in prayer.

There was no official prayerbook until Amram Gaon, of Sura, in Babylonia (846–864), arranged the first Siddur.

Today, we pray at home or in the synagogue, and we use a special prayerbook. This prayerbook is called a Siddur. The Hebrew word *siddur* means "order." The Siddur contains prayers and blessings in Hebrew and in English in a special order.

Today, there are a great number of different Siddurim. The Orthodox, Conservative, Reform, and Reconstructionist movements all publish their own special editions of the Siddur.

In the synagogue the rabbi leads the prayer service. The cantor (*chazan* in Hebrew) is a person with a good singing voice who chants the prayers.

YOUR HEBREW WORD LIST

סִדּוּר	Siddur	Prayerbook
רַבִּי	Rabbi	Teacher, scholar
חַזָּן	Chazan	Cantor
תְּפִלּוֹת	Tefilot	Prayers
אַמְרָם גָּאוֹן	Amram Gaon	Arranged the first Siddur

CHOOSE YOUR ANSWER FROM THE WORD LIST
Write your answer in English or in Hebrew.

1. The prayerbook used in the synagogue on Shabbat is the _____.

2. The Siddur contains _____ and blessings in Hebrew and English.

3. The _____ leads the congregation in prayer and in study.

4. The _____ has a good voice and chants the prayers for the congregation.

5. Rabbi _____ arranged the Siddur.

SEMAPHORE CODE
To decipher this code substitute the letter for the semaphore signal.

START

 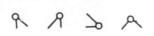 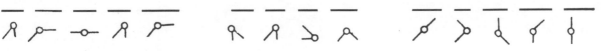

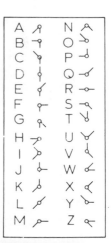

מַעֲרִיב מִנְחָה מוּסָף שַׁחֲרִית·

HOW many different prayer services are there in the Siddur?

EACH of the six days of the week has three prayer services. The morning service is called Shacharit, the afternoon service is called Mincha, and the evening service is called Maariv.

On Shabbat there is an extra prayer service called Musaf, meaning "additional."

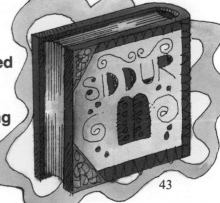

43

SYNAGOGUE BOOKS סִפְרֵי בֵּית־הַכְּנֶסֶת

During the cycle of the Jewish holiday year, we use a variety of special books. Some of them are prayerbooks and some of them are biblical books.

Each and every Sabbath and Jewish holiday we read from the Torah. You follow the Torah and Haftarah reading in a Chumash. Your synagogue Chumash is translated into English, and also has commentaries to explain the text.

What is the name of the Chumash your synagogue uses?

On Rosh Hashanah and Yom Kippur you pray in a special prayer book called a Machzor. The word Machzor comes from the Hebrew word *chazor*, which means "to repeat." The prayers for the High Holy Days are repeated by Jews all over the world. One of the first Machzorim ever compiled was the Machzor Vitry. It was composed by a pupil of Rashi called Rabbi Simha, who lived in Vitry, France.

The Orthodox, Reform, Conservative, and Reconstructionist movements have published their own special Machzorim. What is the name of the Machzor used in your synagogue?

The Siddur is the prayerbook for weekdays and Shabbat. It contains passages from the Bible and the Talmud, as well as prayer selections written by rabbis and poets.

The first official prayerbook was arranged by Amran Gaon of Sura in 846–864. Since that time thousands of different Siddurim have been published. Today, the Orthodox, Conservative, Reform, and Reconstructionist movements have published their own editions of the Siddur. What is the name of your synagogue's Siddur?

During the holiday of Passover we use a special Seder prayerbook called the Haggadah. Some of its contents were part of the Seder services 2,000 years ago. The recital of the Haggadah is the most important part of the Seder service. It tells the story of the Israelites in Egypt and their fight for freedom. More than 3,000 editions of the Haggadah have been published.

YOUR HEBREW WORD LIST

סִדּוּר	**Siddur**	**Prayerbook**
מַחְזוֹר	**Machzor**	**Prayerbook used on High Holy Days**
הַגָּדָה	**Haggadah**	**"The telling" (of the Pesach story)**
חֻמָשׁ	**Chumash**	**The Torah. The Five Books of Moses.**

CHOOSE YOUR ANSWER FROM THE WORD LIST
Write your answer in English or in Hebrew.

1. On Rosh Hashanah we use a special prayerbook called a _____.

2. You follow the Torah and Haftarah readings in your _____.

3. The recital of the _____ is the most important part of the Seder.

4. The prayerbook used on Shabbat and weekdays is called _____.

סְפָרִים קְדוֹשִׁים

ARE there other prayerbooks or biblical texts which are used in the synagogue?

Purim is Megillat Esther time. The Scroll of Esther is the last of the five scrolls in the part of the Bible known as Ketuvim (see p. 52). Megillat Esther tells the story of a Jewish woman who saved the lives of the Jews of Persia. On Purim we read the Scroll of Esther and try to drown out the name of evil Haman with boos and graggers.

On Shavuot we read Megillat Ruth. The Book of Ruth is one of the scrolls in the part of the Bible called Ketuvim. The scroll tells about the love of Ruth, a convert to Judaism, for her mother-in-law, Naomi. The Book of Ruth is read because King David was descended from the marriage of Ruth and Boaz.

During the period between Pesach and Rosh Hashanah some synagogues study Pirke Avot, "Ethics of the Fathers." It was written about 2,000 years ago by the wise rabbis of that period. The text contains many wise sayings and religious teachings.

THE PSALMS תְּהִלִּים

David was a king with many skills. He was a victorious general and defeated the Philistines. He captured the city of Jerusalem and made it the capital of Israel.

David was also an excellent musician. When King Saul was not feeling well David played his harp for him. The music made King Saul feel better. The Bible calls David "the sweet singer of Israel."

The word "psalms" means "a song sung to a stringed instrument." In addition to his other skills, King David was the author of many psalms. These have been collected in the Book of Psalms. The Hebrew name of this book is Tehillim. The Book of Tehillim is a collection of 150 religious poems. Each of them praises God. Many of David's psalms are included in the prayerbook and are recited at services.

PSALM 92: "A Song for the Sabbath"
This prayer is recited during the Sabbath and holiday morning services.

PSALM 95: "Let us sing to God"
This prayer is recited during the Friday evening services.

PSALM 90: "A prayer of Moses"
This prayer is recited on the Sabbath and holidays.

PSALM 96: "Sing to Adonai a new song"
This prayer is recited during the Friday evening services.

Did you know that these prayers are psalms and some were written by King David?

YOUR HEBREW WORD LIST

יְרוּשָׁלַיִם	Yerushalayim	Jerusalem
תְּהִלִּים	Tehillim	Psalms
שִׁיר	Shir	Song
דָּוִד הַמֶּלֶךְ	David ha-Melech	King David
תְּפִלָּה	Tefillah	Prayer

CHOOSE YOUR ANSWER FROM THE WORD LIST
Write your answer in English or in Hebrew.

1. King David was the author of _____.

2. The capital of the ancient kingdom of Israel was _____.

3. The word Tehillim means "a _____ sung on a stringed

4. _____ was the author of the Book of Psalms.

5. The _____ "A Song for the Sabbath" is recited during the Shabbat and holiday services.

HEBREW SPY CODE.
Substitute English letters for the Hebrew and you will decipher the secret message.

START

__ __ __ __ __ __ __ __ __
כ ע נ ג ד א ו ע ד

__ __ __ __ __ __ __ __ __ __ __ __ __ __
ף ר ד ט י ט ח י פ ס א ל מ ס

A	א
B	ב
C	ג
D	ד
E	ה
F	ו
G	ז
H	ח
I	ט
J	י
K	כ
L	ל
M	מ
N	נ
O	ס
P	ע
Q	פ
R	צ
S	ק
T	ר
U	ש
V	ת
W	ך
X	ם
Y	ן
Z	ף

WHAT does the Hebrew word Tehillim mean?

THE TITLE Tehillim means praises. The Psalms are songs of praise which were sung to the sound of musical instruments.

THE TORAH תּוֹרָה

The Torah that Moses gave the Hebrews was written on a parchment scroll. It was written in Hebrew.

The Torah, or Bible, has been translated into more than 1,000 languages. It tells us that there is only one God. It also tells us how to observe the Sabbath and celebrate the Jewish holidays. The Torah also teaches us how to live a peaceful and good life.

The Torah Scroll is divided into five sections, or books. The Hebrew names of these books are Bereshit, Shmot, Vayikra, Bamidbar, and Devarim.

1. A Torah Scroll must be written by hand. The scribe who writes the Torah Scroll is called a Sofer.

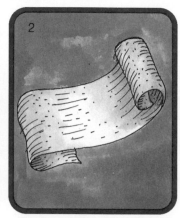

2. As in olden days the Torah is written on parchment. Parchment is made from the skin of a sheep.

3. The Sofer uses a pen made from a goose feather.

4. When the Torah is completed it is attached to two wooden rollers. A roller is called an Etz Hayim.

5. The Torah is dressed with a mantle. Then the Torah is crowned with a silver Keter.

6. Aron Kodesh means "holy ark". The Torah is kept in the Aron Kodesh.

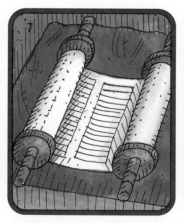

7. Shabbats and holidays are special. The Torah is read in the Synagogue on Shabbats and on holidays.

8. The Torah is divided into fifty-four sections called Sidrot.

YOUR HEBREW WORD LIST

סְדָרוֹת	**Sidrot**	**Weekly Torah portions**
סוֹפֵר	**Sofer**	**Scribe who writes the Torah scroll by hand**
תּוֹרָה	**Torah**	**The Five Books of Moses**
עֵץ חַיִּים	**Etz Chayim**	**Wooden roller**
אֲרוֹן קוֹדֶשׁ	**Aron Kodesh**	**Holy Ark**

CHOOSE YOUR ANSWER FROM THE WORD LIST
Write your answer in English or in Hebrew.

1. A _____ must be written by hand.

2. The person who writes a Torah Scroll is called a _____.

3. The Torah is divided into fifty-four _____.

4. _____ means "Holy Ark."

5. _____ is a wooden roller to which the Torah is attached.

SYMBOL CODE
To decipher this code, substitute the letter for the indicated symbol.

A ⊙	N ♌
B ♃	O ♏
C ♏	P ♎
D ♊	Q ♍
E ♅	R ♐
F ♇	S ♈
G ♀	T ♓
H ♂	U V
I ♀	V ♒
J ☾	W ♉
K ♉	X ♈
L ♈	Y ♊
M ♒	Z <

START

_ _ _   _ _ _ _ _ _   _ _ _

_ _ _ _ _   _ _ _ _   _ _ _ _ _ _

סוֹפֵר

IS A Sofer allowed to write a Torah from memory?

A Sofer must write the Torah from a model copy. He must also follow the rules in the guide for Soferim called Tikkun Soferim.

49

TORAH DICTIONARY מִלוֹן שֶׁל הַתּוֹרָה

TORAH Moses brought the Torah down from Mount Sinai. It contains the Five Books of Moses. The Torah is hand-written with a special alefbet script on parchment.

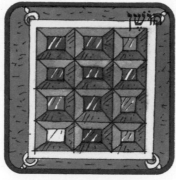

CHOSHEN In biblical times the High Priest's breastplate had twelve precious stones, one for each of the tribes. Today a similar silver ornament is used to beautify the Torah.

KLAF The Torah is written on parchment called Klaf. Thousands of years ago there was no paper, so parchment, made from the skin of animals, was used.

SOFER The person who writes the Torah by hand is called a Sofer. The Sofer writes the Torah according to special rules .

ATZEI CHAYIM These are wooden Torah rollers for the beginning and the end of the Torah scroll.

PAROCHET The embroidered curtain which hangs before the Ark. On the High Holy Days a white Parochet is used.

MAPPAH This is the embroidered mantle used to cover the Torah. It has two openings at the top for the Atzei Chayim.

ARON KODESH The holy Ark which houses the Torah. Because it is so holy it is the most beautiful part of the synagogue.

YAD A pointer used by the Baal Koreh as a guide to reading the Sidrah.

50

KETER A crown usually made of silver. The Keter is an ornament for the top of the Torah.

BAAL KOREH The person who reads the Torah is called the Baal Koreh, or master reader. He or she must be well versed in Hebrew and be able to read the special Torah script without vowels.

YOUR HEBREW WORD LIST

פָּרוֹכֶת	Parochet	Ark curtain
יָד	Yad	Torah pointer
חוֹשֶׁן	Choshen	Torah breastplate
מַפָּה	Mapah	Torah covering
בַּעַל קוֹרֵא	Baal Koreh	Torah reader

CHOOSE YOUR ANSWER FROM THE WORD LIST
Write your answer in English or in Hebrew.

1. The curtain which hangs in front of the Aron Kodesh is called _____.

2. The Baal Koreh uses a _____ as a guide to read the Torah.

3. The person who reads the Torah on the Shabbat and holidays, is called a _____.

4. In biblical times the High Priest wore a breastplate. Today, a similar ornament, called a _____, is used to decorate the Torah.

5. An embroidered _____ was used to cover the Torah.

FIND THE WORD
Unscramble these two story words.

חֲזַק חֲזַק וְנִתְחַזֵּק

WHAT happens when you finish studying one of the books of the Torah?

WHENEVER one of the Five Books of the Torah is completed, the members of the congregation stand up and recite, "Chazak Chazak V'Nitchazek."

This means, "Let us be strong and live according to the rules and teachings of the Torah."

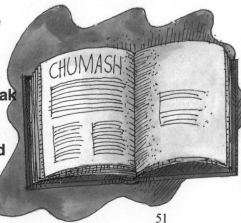

THE TANAK תַּנַ"ךְ

The Hebrew Bible is called TaNaK. The origin of this name is very interesting. The Bible is divided into three parts:

Take the first letter of the name of each part. Put an a between them to help in pronouncing, and now read the five letters as one word. What does it spell? That's right, TaNaK.

The TaNaK consists of 24 separate books.

1. TORAH
The Torah is the first section of the TaNaK. It has 5 books. In the Torah are stories about Abraham and Sarah, Isaac and Rebecca, Jacob and Leah and Rachel. There are also stories about Joseph and Moses.

2. NEVIIM
The Neviim is the second section. It has 8 books. In the Neviim are stories about Joshua, the judges, and the prophets.

3. KETUVIM
The third and last section is the Ketuvim. It has 11 books. They include stories about Ruth, Queen Esther, and Daniel in the lion's den.

The TaNaK is very precious to us. It teaches us about God, to honor our parents and to always tell the truth.

STUDY IT!

Study it carefully, said the rabbis. If you follow the rules in the TaNaK you will live a happy and peaceful life.

YOUR HEBREW WORD LIST

תַּנַ"ךְ	TaNaK	Twenty-four books of the Bible
תּוֹרָה	Torah	Five Books of Moses
נְבִיאִים	Neviim	Prophets
כְּתוּבִים	Ketuvim	Writings

CHOOSE YOUR ANSWER FROM THE WORD LIST
Write your answer in English or in Hebrew.

1. The _____ consists of twenty-four books.

2. The _____ is the first section of the TaNaK.

3. The stories about Queen Esther and Ruth are found in the section of the TaNaK called _____.

4. The second section of the TaNaK is called _____.

DIAL-A-MESSAGE
The first number tells you what circle to look at. The second number tells you which letter to write down. For example: 7-1 is "P" (the first letter on the "7" circle).

START

__ __ __   __ __ __ __ __   __ __ __
8-1 4-2 3-2   8-1 2-1 6-2 2-1 5-2   4-2 2-1 7-3

__ __ __ __ __ __   __ __ __ __
8-1 9-1 3-2 6-2 8-1 9-3   3-3 6-3 8-2 7-2

__ __ __ __ __
2-2 6-3 6-3 5-2 7-3

עַם הַסֵּפֶר

WHY are the Jewish people called the "People of the Book?"

BOOK refers to the Tanak. The Tanak, all 24 books, tells the early history of the Jewish people.

THE HAFTARAH   הַפְטָרָה

All over the world, in all countries, Jews read the same portion (sidrah) of the Torah on holidays and on Shabbat. There are fifty-four portions (sidrot) in the Torah, one for each week of the year. Every week we read a different one.

It takes one year to read the whole Torah. We read the last sidrah on the holiday of Simchat Torah. Then we start over again by reading the first sidrah of the Torah. This shows that the study of the Torah is never finished. Each year we read it again, and again.

On page 52 you learned that the Hebrew Bible of TaNaK is made up of three sections. Every Saturday and holiday we read a sidrah from the Torah, but we don't forget the other section of the TaNaK, the Neviim.

After the rabbi finishes reading the sidrah from the Torah, someone else reads a selection from the second section of the TaNaK. This part of the Torah ceremony is called reading the Haftarah.

The Haftarah readings are from the books you are now studying. The Haftarah readings include stories about Joshua, Samson, Samuel and Ruth.

YOUR HEBREW WORD LIST

תּוֹרָה	Torah	Five Books of Moses
סְדָרוֹת	Sidrot	Weekly Torah portions
הַפְטָרָה	Haftarah	Weekly portion from the Prophets
תַּנַ"ךְ	TaNaK	Twenty-four books of the Bible.
רַבִּי	Rabbi	Scholar, Teacher

CHOOSE YOUR ANSWER FROM THE WORD LIST
Write your answer in English or in Hebrew.

1. After the _____ finishes reading the Sidrah someone else reads the Haftarah.

2. The _____ is made up of three sections: Torah, Neviim, and Ketuvim.

3. The _____ readings include sections from the Neviim and Ketuvim.

4. There are fifty-four _____ in the Torah.

SEMAPHORE CODE
To decipher this code substitute the letter for the semaphore signal.

START

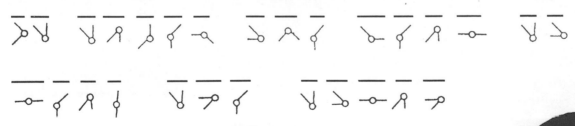

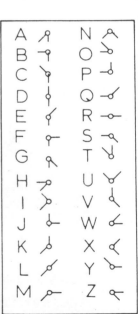

A	⚐	N	⚐
B	⚐	O	⚐
C	⚐	P	⚐
D	⚐	Q	⚐
E	⚐	R	⚐
F	⚐	S	⚐
G	⚐	T	⚐
H	⚐	U	⚐
I	⚐	V	⚐
J	⚐	W	⚐
K	⚐	X	⚐
L	⚐	Y	⚐
M	⚐	Z	⚐

יִישַׁר כֹּחַ

WHAT is the proper way to congratulate a Torah honoree?

WHEN an Aliyah is completed, you congratulate the honoree by shaking his or her hand and saying "Yeshair Koach"—"May you be strengthened."

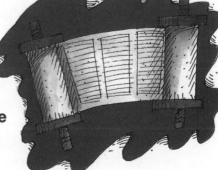

55

ALIYOT עֲלִיּוֹת

The Torah is the special symbol of Judaism. It is read in the synagogue every Shabbat and on every holiday. These weekly and holiday readings make the synagogue the school for learning about our history, our religion, and our ethical laws.

There is a special Torah service in which all members of the congregation take part.

On Shabbat, the Torah service starts in the middle of the Shacharit prayers. The Cantor sings the prayer Ayn Kamocha, and someone is given the honor of opening the Aron Kodesh.

This honor is called P'teechah ("the opening").

The honoree opens the Ark and removes the sacred Torah. The honoree hands the Torah to the Cantor. Now the Cantor and the honoree march around the synagogue so that everyone can see and touch the Torah.

The Torah is brought up to the Beemah so that the Baal Koreh can read it. During the Torah reading seven people are given honors. They recite a blessing before their portion is read and another blessing after the portion is finished.

In some synagogues a Kohen and a Levi are given the first two honors.

After each reading, a Me Sheberach is recited. This prayer blesses the members of the honoree's family, friends, and relatives.

The last person called to the Torah is for the Maftir portion of the Sidrah. This person is called Baal Maftir. The Baal Maftir reads the Haftarah, which is usually related to the Torah reading.

When the reading is all finished, two more honors are given. A strong person is called to receive the honor of Hagbah ("lifting"). The person lifts up the Torah and shows it to the congregation.

The next honoree is called G'leelah ("rolling up"). This person rolls up the Torah and dresses it up again with its mantle and its silver ornaments.

The person who received the honor of opening the Ark and removing the Torah also gets the honor of returning it.

YOUR HEBREW WORD LIST

גְּלִילָה	G'leelah	Rolling
פְּתִיחָה	P'teechah	Opening
בַּעַל מַפְטִיר	Baal Maftir	Maftir reader
מִי שֶׁבֵּרַךְ	Me Sheberach	"May God Bless"
הַגְבָּהָה	Hagbah	Lifting

CHOOSE YOUR ANSWER FROM THE WORD LIST

Write your answer in English or in Hebrew.

1. The honor of opening the Aron Kodesh is called _____.

2. After each reading a _____ prayer is recited. This prayer blesses the honoree's family.

3. The honor of lifting the Torah is called _____.

4. The honor of rolling and dressing the Torah is called _____.

5. The person who reads the Haftarah is called the _____.

SEMAPHORE CODE

To decipher this code substitute the letter for the semaphore signal.

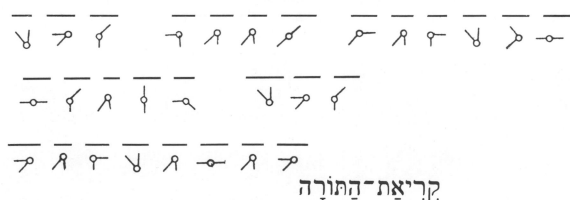

קְרִיאַת־הַתּוֹרָה

IS THE Torah read on the Jewish holidays?

YES! The Torah is read on Shabbat and also on Jewish holidays. On every holiday, special sections of the Torah are read. These selections deal with the subject and history of that particular holiday.

THE MEFORSHIM הַמְּפָרְשִׁים

The TaNaK consists of twenty-four books all written during different periods of Jewish history. It is a library of subjects which teach us much about our beginnings and our religion. The TaNaK contains sections on history, laws, prophecy, prayers, and advice.

The TaNaK was written thousands of years ago before the invention of paper, typewriters, and computers. Everything was written by hand on parchment scrolls. The writers tried to save time and space by writing short sentences with very few details. This makes some of the stories in the TaNaK hard to understand. So along came a group of wise people, called commentators, who tried to explain and help us understand some of the difficult passages.

Commentators are called Meforshim in Hebrew. They brought knowledge and information that they had learned from their study of science, mathematics, and languages. These explanations, called commentaries, helped answer some of the questions people had about the stories in the TaNaK. Here are four of the most famous Bible commentators;

Onkelos (second century C.E.) was a convert to Judaism. He translated the Torah into Aramaic. The rabbis ruled that everyone should review the weekly Torah portion twice in Hebrew and once in Aramaic—the translation of Onkelos.

Radak (1160–1235), whose full name was Rabbi David Kimchi, authored a Bible dictionary, a Hebrew grammar, and commentaries on the Prophets and the Psalms. These commentaries were also translated into Latin.

Rashi (1040–1125) is the most famous of the Meforshim. His full name was Rabbi Shlomo Yitzhaki. Rashi explained some of the difficult words by giving their French translation. Rashi's commentaries are printed in a special style of writing called Rashi script.

Ralbag (1288–1344), whose full name was Rabbi Levi Ben Gershon, is also known as Gersonides. Ralbag was a mathematician, a philosopher, an astronomer, and an inventor. He invented an instrument that helped Columbus to discover America.

YOUR HEBREW WORD LIST

רַשִׁ״י	Rashi	Rabbi Shlomo Yitzḥaki
מְפָרְשִׁים	Meforshim	Commentators
אוּנְקְלוֹס	Onkelos	Translated the Torah into Aramaic
רַדַּ״ק	Radak	Rabbi David Kimchi
רַלְבַּ״ג	Ralbag	Gersonides

CHOOSE YOUR ANSWER FROM THE WORD LIST
Write your answer in English or in Hebrew.

1. The commentaries of _____ were printed in a new style of writing.

2. Scholars who write explanations of the Torah text are called _____.

3. _____ was a convert to Judaism. He wrote his comments in Aramaic.

4. The commentaries of _____ were translated into Latin.

5. Rabbi Levi ben Gershon's shortened name is _____.

כְּתָב רַשִׁי

Check the Chumash used in your synagogue. You will find commentaries by these famous Meforshim. See if you can find the names of other commentators.

HOW were the Hebrew commentaries written by the Meforshim?

THE COMMENTARIES are printed in a special style known as Rashi script. Here is the alefbet in Rashi script and in ordinary letters.

ת שׁ ר ק צ פ ע ס נ מ ל כ י ט ח ז ו ה ד ג ב א

ת שׁ ר ק צ פ ע ס נ מ ל כ י ט ח ז ו ה ד ג ב א

Now read this inscription.

מַזָּל טוֹב

BABY NAMING שִׂמְחַת הַשֵּׁם

Your parents were very happy when you were born. Your grandparents, relatives, and friends visited you at the hospital. Everyone agreed you were the most beautiful and smartest baby they had ever seen. But you had no name and you were just a baby.

Your parents spent a lot of time debating and choosing two names for you.

Different Jewish groups have special ways of choosing a Hebrew name.

Ashkenazi Jews (from Northern Europe) name their children after a close relative who has died.

Sephardic Jews (from Arab countries) name their children after a close relative who is alive and well.

Jewish children have two names; an English name and a Hebrew name. Once your parents decided, you were given your Hebrew name at a special baby-naming service in the synagogue.

If you are a boy, your Hebrew name is followed by the word *ben* ("son "), followed by your father's and mother's Hebrew names.

If you are a girl, your Hebrew name is followed by the word *bat* ("daughter "), followed by the Hebrew names of your father and mother.

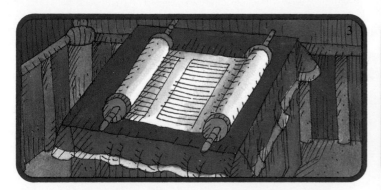

Your parents brought you to the synagogue for the service, and they were called to the Torah and given an Aliyah. After the recitation of the Torah blessings, the rabbi blessed you and gave you your Hebrew name.

Even though you were tiny, you knew exactly what was happening. You were so happy you smiled all through the ceremony. You also gave a tiny burp to show you liked your Hebrew name.

What is your Hebrew name?

After whom were you named?

YOUR HEBREW WORD LIST

בֵּן	Ben	Son
בַּת	Bat	Daughter
עֲלִיָּה	Aliyah	"Going up" to honor the Torah
הוֹרִים	Horim	Parents
שֵׁם	Shem	Name

CHOOSE YOUR ANSWER FROM THE WORD LIST
Write your answer in English or in Hebrew.

1. If the child is a boy, its Hebrew name is followed by the word _____.

2. If the child is a girl, its Hebrew name is followed by the word _____.

3. People who are called to the Torah are given a _____.

4. Sephardic Jews give their children a _____ after a close relative who is alive.

5. The _____ of a newborn child are honored with an Aliyah.

HEBREW SPY CODE.
Substitute English letters for the Hebrew.

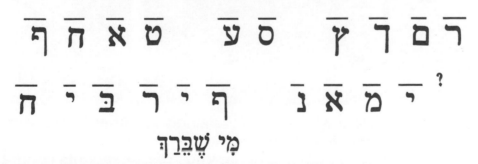

START

ף ח א ט ע ס ץ ד מ ר

ח י ר ב י ף נ א מ י ?

מִי שֶׁבֵּרַךְ

A	א ב
B	
C	ה ד
D	ו
E	י
F	שׁ
G	ג
H	ח
I	ט
J	כ
K	ל
L	מ
M	ג
N	ם
O	פ
P	ף
Q	ק
R	ר
S	ס
T	ט
U	ם
V	ן
W	ז
X	ט
Y	ז
Z	צ

IS THERE a special prayer that is recited at the baby-naming service? THE RABBI recites a Me Sheberach prayer at the baby-naming service.

Mesheberach means "May God bless." In this prayer the parents, as well as the newborn child, are blessed.

After the Me Sheberach blessing, the ceremony continues and the child is given its Hebrew name.

BAR–BAT MITZVAH בַּר־מִצְוָה בַּת־מִצְוָה

As you grow older, you become smarter and are able to accept more responsibilities. Your parents give you important things to do. Neighbors and friends trust you, and ask you to babysit for them. You are growing up real fast.

Long ago, the rabbis decided that at the age of thirteen Jewish boys and girls were ready and able to accept religious responsibilities. Today, at the age of thirteen a Jewish boy or girl becomes Bar or Bat Mitzvat.

Bar is the Hebrew word for "son." Bar Mitzvah means "son of the commandment." Bat is the Hebrew word for "daughter." Bat Mitzvah means "daughter of the commandment."

It is a time when you get an Aliyah to the Torah. It is also a time when you give your own Tzedakah. When you become Bar or Bat Mitzvah, you can also become a part of a minyan.

Bar or Bat Mitzvah is much more than a big ceremony and a party. Several months before, you start to learn your Maftir and Haftarah.

When the happy Shabbat arrives, you are called to the Torah. You walk up to the reading desk a little shaky, and you sing the blessings and chant the Haftarah. If you study real hard, the rabbi will also let you read the Torah section, the Maftir.

Your whole family, relatives and friends, are in the synagogue to honor you. Sometimes, you even get to give a sermon, just like the rabbi.

Of course, it is just a little shorter.

After the service there is a great big celebration, and everyone congratulates you on your Torah reading and your great speech.

MAZAL TOV! You are now a Jew, with full religious responsibilities.

YOUR HEBREW WORD LIST

הַפְטָרָה	**Haftarah**	Weekly portion from the Prophets
בַּר־מִצְוָה	**Bar Mitzvah**	Temple ceremony for boy at age thirteen
בַּת־מִצְוָה	**Bat Mitzvah**	Temple ceremony for girl at age thirteen
מַפְטִיר	**Maftir**	Torah reading by Bar or Bat Mitzvah
עֲלִיָּה	**Aliyah**	"Going up" to honor the Torah

CHOOSE YOUR ANSWER FROM THE WORD LIST
Write your answer in English or in Hebrew.

1. Boys become _____ when they reach the age of thirteen.

2. Girls become _____ when they reach the age of thirteen.

3. The _____ is from the Prophets and the Writings.

4. A person who is called to the Torah is given a _____.

5. The Bar and Bat Mitzvah Torah reading is called _____.

SYMBOL CODE

To decipher this code, substitute the letter for the indicated symbol.

START

_ _ _   _ _ _ _   _ _ _ _ _   _ _ _

_ _ _ _ _   _   _ _ _ _ _ _ _ ?

A ⊙	N ♌
B ♃	O ♏
C ♄	P ♎
D ♂	Q ♍
E ♅	R ♐
F ♆	S ♒
G ♀	T ♓
H ♂	U ∨
I ☿	V ≈
J ☾	W >
K ♃	X ≫
L ‖	Y ⊥
M ♌	Z <

WHERE does the idea of Bar and Bat Mitzvah come from?

IN THE Talmud, Rabbi Judah ben Tema said, "a child of thirteen is responsible for fulfilling the commandments."

JEWISH WEDDING קִדּוּשִׁין

The greatest joy for parents is to see their children grow up into healthy, happy, worthwhile men and women. This is exactly what your parents, your rabbi, and your teachers wish for you. Someday you will grow up and meet a nice Jewish boy/girl and get married. Then you will have children, and do the same thing for your sons and daughters. This is God's plan for the human family.

The sages use the Hebrew word *kiddushin* ("holy") to mean marriage. A Jewish wedding is a holy event. It is also the happiest event in the Jewish life-cycle.

On the Saturday before the wedding, the bride and the bridegroom are called to the Torah and given an Aliyah. In Yiddish this Aliyah is called Aufruf. If possible, both families attend the Aufruf ceremony. Some of them are also given Aliyot.

The bride and bridegroom stand under a Chuppah (marriage canopy) decorated with flowers and ribbons. They are escorted by the families to the Chuppah.

The rabbi recites the blessing over a cup of wine, and the bride and bridegroom sip some of the wine and exchange rings.

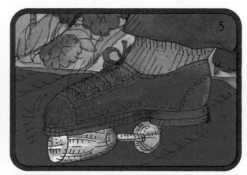

Following this, the Ketubah (marriage contract) is read out loud. Originally the Ketubah was written in Aramaic. Today, some are written in Hebrew.

After the Ketubah is read, seven blessings are recited. Some of the wedding guests are given the honor of reciting a blessing.

The Kiddushin closes with the crushing of a wine glass under the foot of the groom. This ceremony is a reminder of the destruction of the Holy Temple in Jerusalem.

After the ceremony, the guests shout Mazal Tov and sing at the top of their lungs. Of course, there is a great big feast with lots of good food, gooey desserts, and much dancing and fun.

YOUR HEBREW WORD LIST

כַּלָּה	Kalah	Bride
חָתָן	Chatan	Groom
כְּתוּבָּה	Ketubah	Marriage certificate
חֻפָּה	Chuppah	Wedding Canopy
עֲלִיָּה	Aliyah	"Going up" to honor the Torah

CHOOSE YOUR ANSWER FROM THE WORD LIST
Write your answer in English or in Hebrew.

1. A Jewish marriage contract is called a _____.

2. Before the wedding the bride and bridegroom are called to the Torah and given a _____.

3. The bride and bridegroom stand under a _____ decorated with flowers and ribbons.

4. The _____ and _____ sip wine and recite the blessings and exchange wedding rings.

FIND THE WORD
Unscramble these two story words.

מַזָּל טוֹב

HOW do you congratulate the newly-weds after the wedding?

AFTER the wedding ceremony you approach the bride and groom and wish them "Mazal Tov"—good luck. You also greet the members of the family with the same salutation.

TZEDAKAH צְדָקָה

Tzedakah is not a special ceremony that is performed only on the holidays or at special fund-raising events. The mitzvah of Tzedakah is a daily function in the cycle of everyday Jewish living. Giving Tzedakah is a great mitzvah. In fact, one of the rabbis quoted in the Talmud, Rav Assi, said, "Charity is equal to all mitzvot."

Your ancestors were farmers in the land of Isarel. They left wheat, corn, and all kinds of fruits in the fields for the poor and the needy.

In addition there was a special tithe called *maasar oni* ("poor tax"), which the farmers set aside for the poor. Every third year the farmer donated one-tenth of the crop to the needy.

The Holy Temple in Jerusalem had a special room called "Tzedakah room" which was kept very dark. In this way rich people could leave their donation and the poor could receive help without being embarrassed or shamed because of their poverty.

When your ancestors were driven out of the land of Israel they carried their ideals of Tzedakah with them. Wherever they settled your ancestors set up Tzedakah societies. These groups educated the children, visited the sick, sheltered the aged, buried the poor, and provided ransoms for kidnapped prisoners.

Jews keep Tzedakah boxes, called pushkes in Yiddish, in their homes. Many have made it a tradition to put money in the pushke before lighting Shabbat candles each Friday night. That's the sort of tradition that you could start in your home too. You can contribute to Israel, to many Jewish causes, and to other worthy causes. It doesn't really matter how much you give, but how you give is important.

Today, the Jewish community in America carries on the Jewish tradition of Tzedakah on a large national and international scale. The Jewish Federation and similar organizations support many institutions, such as schools, old age homes, hospitals, and community centers in America and overseas.

YOUR HEBREW WORD LIST

מִצְוָה	Mitzvah	A good deed, commandment
צְדָקָה	Tzedakah	Charity, righteousness
בֵּית־הַמִּקְדָּשׁ	Bet Hamikdash	The Holy Temple
פּוּשְׁקֶע	Pushke	Charity box
מַעֲשָׂר עוֹנִי	Maasar Oni	Tithe

CHOOSE YOUR ANSWER FROM THE WORD LIST
Write your answer in English or in Hebrew.

1. Every third year the farmers in Israel set aside a special _____ for the poor.

2. The Yiddish name for a Tzedakah box is _____.

3. Wherever Jews settled, they set up _____ societies.

4. Giving Tzedakah is a great _____.

5. The _____ had a special Tzedakah room.

מַעֲשִׂים טוֹבִים

WHAT is the ladder of Tzedakah?

MAIMONIDES, the great scholar, put the Jewish ideas about how to give charity into a simple code called the "Ladder of Tzedakah." It tells us the eight degrees of giving charity. It explains the best ways to give Tzedakah.

There are eight degrees of charity, starting with the most important:
1. Helping someone to help himself.
2. Giving anonymously to an unknown person.
3. Giving anonymously to a person you know is in need.
4. Giving without knowing who will get the gift.
5. Giving without being asked.
6. Giving after being asked.
7. Giving less than one can afford, but giving willingly.
8. Giving unwillingly.

TARYAG MITZVOT תַּרְיַ"ג מִצְוֹת

According to Maimonides, there are 613 mitzvot in the Torah. The Hebrew letters whose numerical value equals 613 spell out the word Taryag, so we call these the Taryag mitzvot.

There are 248 yes-do mitzvot. These are mitzvot that God wants us to do, such as praying and honoring our parents.
In Hebrew these are called *mitzvot aseh*.
There are 365 mitzvot that are the don't-do kind. These are called *mitzvot lo taaseh*. Don't steal and don't kill are just two examples.

There are mitzvot associated with every part of your life: how you behave in school and how you play sports, how you treat your friends and family. Mitzvot are a part of the cycle of your Jewish life: birth, Bar Mitzvah/Bat Mitzvah, wedding, and death.
There are mitzvot about the food you eat and how you will act as a grown-up in business or in your profession.

248+
365=
613

One mitzvah leads to another. For example, when you help someone, you may feel so good inside that before you know it you find yourself helping someone else! Or when your family has a Passover Seder, they may also do the mitzvah of inviting a guest to share the holiday with them.
The more mitzvot you do, the more you follow God's will, and you will be happier for it.

You might not know it, but study is a mitzvah too, and a very important one. Parents and teachers used to give children honey cakes or drops of honey on the day their studies began. This showed the children that the study of the Torah is sweet and encouraged them to learn. Study is so important because it helps us to learn God's will. When we study the Torah, we learn about more mitzvot that we can do.

YOUR HEBREW WORD LIST

תּוֹרָה	Torah	The Five Books of Moses
מִצְווֹת	Mitzvot	Good deeds, Commandments
מִצְוַת עֲשֵׂה	Mitzvah aseh	Yes-do Mitzvah
מִצְוַת לֹא תַעֲשֶׂה	Mitzvah lo taaseh	Don't-do mitzvah
תַּרְיַ"ג	Taryag	613 Mitzvot

CHOOSE YOUR ANSWER FROM THE WORD LIST
Write your answer in English or in Hebrew.

1. There are _____ mitzvot in the Torah.

2. 365 _____ are of the "don't-do" kind.

3. Don't-do mitzvot are called _____ in Hebrew.

4. The mitzvot that God wants us to do are called _____.

5. _____ study is a mitzvah.

HEBREW SPY CODE.
Substitute English letters for the Hebrew and you will decipher the secret message.

START

ט א ר ץ א ג   מ י א נ ס

ס ע ז   ח נ מ ד ר י ד

א נ ד   ט ע ר ט י י נ

A	א
B	ב
C	ד
D	י
E	ש
F	ג
G	ה
H	ח
I	ת
J	כ
K	ל
L	מ
M	נ
N	ג
O	ן
P	פ
Q	ק
R	ר
S	ס
T	ט
U	ם
V	ו
W	ז
X	ע
Y	ץ
Z	צ

69

A TIME TO DIE מָוֶת

Each of us is surrounded by a circle of parents, grandparents, relatives, and good friends. These people love us, care for us, play with us, protect us, and teach us.

Sometimes something sad happens to this friendly circle of protectors. Sometimes, someone you love, respect, and care for dies. It is a sad, painful, and puzzling time. But there is nothing anyone can do about death. It is the final part in the cycle of life.

Jewish funerals are short and simple. The rabbi delivers a short eulogy about the person. This eulogy is called a Hespad in Hebrew. After the Hespad the rabbi recites psalms and the prayer El Maleh Rachamim, "O merciful God."

When the Hespad is finished, the rabbi approaches the mourners and makes a cut in their jacket or attaches a black ribbon. This ritual is called Kreah, which means "cutting."

At the cemetery the coffin is lowered into the grave. Each of the members of the funeral party sadly throws some earth into the grave. It is a mitzvah to participate in a funeral

At the graveside, the members of the family recite the Kaddish. The Kaddish prayer is written in Aramaic.

It is customary for the mourners to sit on low stools as relatives and friends visit and comfort them. This is called "sitting shivah". Shivah means seven. Some people "sit" for seven days.

The anniversary of the person's death is called Yahrzeit. At the same time each year the mourners recite the Kaddish and light a Yahrzeit candle. In this way we remember and honor the memory of the person.

A year after the person's death a tombstone, Matzevah, is set over the grave. The inscription includes the dates of birth and death as well as the Hebrew/English name of the deceased.

YOUR HEBREW WORD LIST

קֶבֶר	Kever	Grave
קְרִיעָה	Kreah	Tearing, cutting
קַדִּישׁ	Kaddish	Prayer for the dead.
מַצֵּבָה	Matzevah	Tombstone
הֶסְפֵּד	Hespad	Eulogy

CHOOSE YOUR ANSWER FROM THE WORD LIST
Write your answer in English or in Hebrew.

1. At the funeral the rabbi delivers a special talk called a _____ about the person who has died.

2. The tearing of a mourner's garment is called _____.

3. After a year it is customary to place a _____ on the grave of the person who died.

4. The family of the deceased recites the _____ at the cemetery.

שִׁבְעָה   יִזְכּוֹר

WHAT do you do when you enter the house of a mourner?

VISITING a mourner during Shivah is a mitzvah. By showing support and concern you help ease the pain of loss.

As you enter the house you will notice that the mourners are seated on low stools or benches. It is a custom not to speak to the mourner until he or she speaks to you. After you express your concern and reminisce about the deceased, you are ready to leave.

When you leave, it is customary to say the following words in Hebrew: "

הַמָּקוֹם יְנַחֵם אֶתְכֶם.   May God comfort you.

WHY AND WHEN is the Yizkor memorial prayer recited?

YIZKOR is recited on Yom Kippur Shemini Atzeret, Passover, and Shavuot. The recitation of the Yizkor prayer helps the family members to remember the loved ones and their way of life.

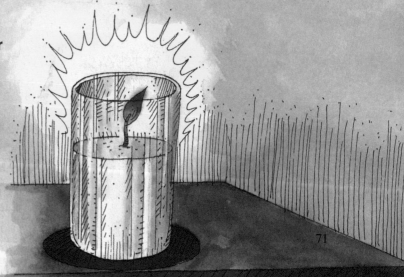

71

PUZZLE ANSWERS